Gentle Ben

This edition is published by special arrangement with Dutton Children's Books, A Division of Penguin Young Readers Group, A Member of Penguin Books (USA) Inc.

Grateful acknowledgment is made to Dutton Children's Books, A Division of Penguin Young Readers Group, A Member of Penguin Books (USA) Inc. for permission to reprint *Gentle Ben* by Walt Morey, illustrated by John Schoenherr, cover illustration by Lori Thorn. Copyright © 1965 by Walt Morey.

Printed in the United States of America

ISBN 10 0-15-365155-5
ISBN 13 978-0-15-365155-7

1 2 3 4 5 6 7 8 9 10   947   17 16 14 13 12 11 10 09 08 07 06

Gentle Ben

By WALT MOREY

Illustrated by
JOHN SCHOENHERR

Strange bedfellows . . .

Mr. Andersen found Mark and Ben in the boulder field. He stepped from the high grass and there they were, not twenty feet in front of him. He pulled up short, the gun halfway to his shoulder. Mark and Ben's friendship had prepared him for something unusual. But not this.

"Holy mackerel!" he gasped under his breath. "Will you look at that!"

Mark half-lay, his shoulders propped against a rock, half-asleep. Ben was stretched out beside him, his big head flat on outstretched forepaws. One paw with its long, cruelly studded claws was actually resting against Mark's leg. Mark's arm lay along Ben's neck, fingers buried in the coarse fur.

Andersen wet his dry lips. Making his voice as quiet, as completely toneless as possible, he called, "Mark. Mark. Wake up."

Mark opened his eyes, blinking at the bright sunlight. Then he saw his father with a rifle. He started up, crying, "No! No! Dad. Please don't."

"Told with a simplicity and dignity which befits its characters, human and animal . . . Mr. Morey has written a vivid chronicle of Alaska, its people and places, challenges and beauties."

—*Library Journal*

"Every step in the remarkable relationship between boy and bear is traced with conviction." —*Book Week*

ILLUSTRATIONS

AUTHOR'S NOTE

THE setting of this story is Alaska before statehood, when it was still a Territory and America's last great frontier. It is a land of violent contrasts, of flowers and strawberries growing in the valleys, and of giant glaciers hanging menacingly over those valleys, of timbered forests and brushlands and rugged mountain ranges, and of barren miles of tundra stretching away without a rise or a break to mar its flatness, a land of hot summer days and stillness a hundred miles deep, a land of shrieking gales, and cold that cuts to the bone. It is a land where people still travel by dog team and canoe, but also where the prospector in the most remote backwoods will fly by the most modern plane.

The people who lived there were, by necessity, a tough and hardy lot, as the first settlers in a new country always are. There is no Orca City as such. But its description could fit any one of a dozen fishing villages along the coast. Because fish piracy was so common before statehood that it was almost recognized as a legitimate business, the battles between the cannery people and the pirates were numerous and often fatal. Laws were so lax that old-timers often said, "In the North, if you really want to, you can get away with anything you're man enough to do."

WALT MOREY

EACH day Mark Andersen told himself he would not stop that night. He would walk right by the shed and not even glance inside. But about two o'clock every afternoon he'd begin thinking of stopping, and the next thing he realized, there he was, his schoolbooks in one hand, a paper bag in the other, staring into the yawning black mouth of the doorway. He knew what would happen if his father learned of it. He feared his father's anger more than anything else. But his desire to enter the shed was so great it drove his fear into the back of his mind, where it gnawed at him like a mouse in a wall.

He squinted his eyes, concentrating on the house several hundred yards down the trail. His mother was not in the yard or in the kitchen window that faced in his direction. She had not waved to him on his way home from school for several weeks now. He had a vague feeling that somehow this fact was important. He worried about it for a moment. Then he turned toward the black interior of the shed, and forgot all else.

"Just once more," he told himself. "This is the last time."

He stepped into the cool, musty dimness, and was momentarily blinded. He stood perfectly still, waiting, listening. He heard the soft pad of feet, the dry rustle of straw, the rattle of a chain. A heavy body brushed against him, almost upsetting him. The next moment the paper bag was almost ripped from his hand.

His exploring hand touched coarse fur, a broad head, a pair

of stubby tulip-shaped ears. When his eyes became accustomed to the gloom, he made out the great blocky shape of the bear. He put both arms about its huge neck, and murmured, "I almost didn't come today. I sure am glad to see you, Ben." Ben twisted his big head, trying to reach the sack. Mark said, "All right, but wait a minute."

Ben was fastened with a chain about his neck; the other end was tied to a post in the center of the building. Because the chain was so short that he could not reach the door or the sunlight, most of his five years had been spent in the building's inner gloom.

Mark went to the post, untied the chain, and transferred it to another supporting post nearer the door so that Ben could get some sunlight while he was there. Before Mark left, he always retied the chain to the center post, just as it had been, so Fog Benson would never guess anyone had been there.

Mark disliked Fog Benson. He always looked dirty. He spent most of his time in the bars, where he talked loud, bragged, and was quarrelsome. Mark's father had said he was sure that Benson was a fish pirate. Mark knew he was mean to Ben. He always kept the bear chained, and sometimes he didn't feed him for days. Then maybe he'd just throw a loaf of stale bread onto the floor.

Mark never worried about Benson finding him in the shed. Fog, like every other man who owned a seine boat, was busy getting it ready for the approaching salmon season.

Ben padded to the end of the chain and stood in the open doorway. It was a warm day, and sky and land were as bright as a new belt buckle. Ben blinked his little eyes at the bright sunlight. He swung his big head right and left as his delicate nostrils eagerly sampled the fresh spring air. Ben was not yet a full-grown brown bear, and he was painfully thin and bony

10

from lack of enough food for his huge frame. Even so, he was a tremendous animal, with great ropes of muscles rippling sinuously under his light taffy-gold coat.

Mark sat down in the sun-drenched doorway and began opening the paper bag. "I saved one of my sandwiches for you, and a couple of the kids didn't eat all theirs so I brought them along, too."

Ben tried to get his big black nose into the sack, and Mark pushed it away. He hit the back of Ben's front legs just above his feet and said, "Down! Sit down, Ben." He patted the floor beside him. Ben stretched out, big forepaws extended. Mark didn't know how he had taught Ben that, or even if he had. But Ben always lay down when Mark did it.

Mark tore the sandwiches into chunks and held them in his palm. Ben lifted the pieces so deftly Mark scarcely felt his tongue. The bear ate them with a great smacking of lips. When it was all gone, Ben pushed at his hand, looking for more. Mark gave him the empty sack, and Ben ripped it apart, snorting and huffing at the aroma that remained. When he was satisfied there was no more, he dropped his big head on his forepaws and lay looking out at the bright spring day.

Mark wished suddenly that Jamie was here so he could share Ben. Jamie had been almost two years older, and much bigger and stronger. It had always been Jamie who thought of the things they should do and the places to go. He still missed Jamie. He guessed he always would. "Jamie would have liked you, too," he said to Ben, and rubbed the fur under his chin.

Ben stretched his neck, closed his eyes, and grunted like a pig, in pure ecstasy. Mark leaned back against Ben's solid side, one arm lying along his neck. His fingers scratched idly at the base of Ben's tulip-shaped ears. Ben twisted his head so Mark could scratch first one ear, then the other.

"I bet you wish you were out there where you could get some of that long green grass and roots and skunk cabbage," Mark said. "This is spring, and bears need that kind of food to prepare their stomachs for summer. I guess you've never had those things." Of course, he knew Ben hadn't. Fog Benson had captured him when the cub was six months old. He had killed Ben's mother and brought the young bear to town to show him off. And because Ben had cried for hours for his lost mother, Fog had laughingly named him "Squeaky Ben," after a local character with a querulous voice. As the cub grew and it became apparent his size would be tremendous, the "Squeaky" part was dropped.

"If you were mine," Mark reflected, "I'd take you down to that stream just beyond the flat. The grass is half as high as I am, and there's lots of roots and things. There's rocks, too. And we'd turn some over and you could eat the grubs and mice under them. If you were mine—"

Mark had been saying this to himself since the first night he had stopped to see Ben. He often lay in bed thinking of it before going to sleep. And he thought of it in school, too. He had got a poor grade in spelling the other day just because he'd been planning his visit to Ben.

After school Miss Taylor had talked to him about the spelling. She had his paper on her desk and was looking at it, shaking her head. "Mark," she said, "you didn't even write down half those spelling words. I'm sure you knew them, so that's not the reason. You were daydreaming again, Mark. You've been doing a lot of that lately. Is there something wrong?"

"Oh, no," he said hastily, "I was just—just thinking."

She said gently, "I know it's spring and there are only two weeks of school left; but try to pay closer attention, Mark."

Several times Mark had thought briefly of suggesting to his

12

Mark leaned back against Ben's solid side.

father that he buy Ben. Fog Benson would probably be glad to get rid of the bear, judging by the way he neglected him. But if Mark hinted at such a thing, he would have to admit he had been stopping to see Ben, and his father's anger was a thing Mark did not want to face.

He wanted to be friends with his father and feel that same closeness there had been between his father and Jamie. Jamie would have been a big man. He had gone on the boat that last summer, and Mark had listened enviously as Jamie and his father discussed fishing and boating problems in man-to-man fashion. But he could never do that. He was not going to be big. And he was afraid of his father's temper, the harshness of his voice. The look from his father's blue eyes when he was displeased could freeze you inside. Mark was sure he would never know such warm companionship with his father. Jamie had got it all. He wondered what would have happened if Jamie had asked for Ben.

Mark rubbed his cheek against Ben's broad forehead, hard as rock covered with fur, and said: "If you were mine I'd feed you up until you were as round as a seal. You'd grow and grow until you were the biggest bear in the whole world, I bet. And I'd train you to walk right behind me all the time. In the summer we could go down to the dock and watch the cruise ships come in, and the people would 'Oh' and 'Ah!' at us, and take pictures. And you'd follow me around like a dog—" At this, Mark paused, struck to his very heart with joy at the thought of arousing such love and devotion in what would be the biggest bear in the whole world. Wouldn't that be something! he thought blissfully. I bet I'd be the only kid in the whole world who had a bear for a pet. Gee!

He snuggled his thin shoulders tighter against Ben's broad, solid side. He was tired. It seemed like he was always tired.

And the warm sun soaking into him made him a little drowsy. He watched the sun through half-closed lids as it dropped toward a white peak. It was going to land right on top like a marble on a mountain. He'd have to go soon. He had to get home before his father. Mother had never asked what made him late, but Dad would.

Off to his left the green and yellow tundra stretched away in gentle rolls and hollows that were broken here and there by the darker green of patches of brush and a ragged line where the creek cut through to the sea. The tundra looked dewy fresh and clean from its long winter under the snow. In the distance the Aleutian Range reared a row of white heads into the blue. Already the snow had melted from the beaches and surrounding lowlands. As the hours of daylight lengthened, the snow line crept farther away. It crept up valleys and canyons, across slopes and razor-sharp ridges until, by the time summer arrived, it would have retreated to that range of white heads, where it would stop.

Below, on his right, lay the uneven roofs of homes and stores of the fishing village of Orca City. Its one mud street, black and drying under the warm sun, slashed straight through the center of town to the bay and the sea, which stretched away, flat and endless, to the distant horizon.

A dozen boats lay at the dock, but the outreaching sea was empty. Soon it would not be. The opening of the Alaskan Salmon Run was but two weeks away, and excitement was beginning to grip the town like a fever. Mark knew about that; his father was a seiner, and his boat, the *Far North,* was one of the finest seiners in Alaska.

Everyone in Orca City made his living from the salmon run in one form or another. "Take the salmon run away," his father once said, "and Orca City would be a ghost town in a

15

month." Naturally, everyone became more excited as opening day drew nearer. Fishing boats would begin to arrive any day now, and Orca City would fill with strange men who had come north to work in the seven canneries along the coast and aboard the fish traps. Soon, more than a thousand seiners from as far south as California and even Mexico would be moored in the bay. Orca City's three or four hundred people would swell to several thousand.

Even now repair crews were making the canneries ready. Aboard boats men were working feverishly, overhauling fishing gear, repairing motors, getting their boats seaworthy. Huge floating fish traps, made of logs and chicken wire, that would catch hundreds of thousands of salmon in a few weeks were being towed to locations at sea where they would be held in place with great anchors. Other traps, made of pilings and wire, were being built right on the trap sites at sea. All day and night the *whoosh-stomp* of pile drivers would be heard up and down the coast as they sank hundred-foot pilings deep into the bottom of the sea to form the shape of a trap.

Like a sprinter crouched in the starting blocks and awaiting the gun, Mark thought, everyone was getting set for the morning the Bureau of Fisheries would announce the opening of the season. Then boats would begin scouring the sea, hunting schools of salmon. The canneries' doors would swing wide. Aboard the traps watchmen would close the "Sunday apron," the wire door that let the salmon escape from the trap back to sea before the season opened. The Alaskan Salmon Run would be officially on.

The brown bears, lean-flanked and rough-coated from their long winter's sleep, would amble down off the high snow fields and congregate along the spawning streams. There would be colossal battles for choice fishing sites; but once those were

16

decided, the animals would all settle down to eating their fill every day as the returning salmon fought their way upstream to spawn. Herds of seals and sea lions would mass on jutting points of land and along rocky shores of islands to dip into the run for their annual feast. They would charge into the nets of seiners, ripping them to shreds, and spend hours searching for the opening to a fish trap, trying to get at the thousands of salmon inside. Eagles, hawks, crows, and foxes would vie with the brown bears, seals, and sea lions at every stream and sandbar. Over all would circle hordes of screaming gulls scouring land, sea, and the beaches, cleaning up, to the last morsel, every crumb left by previous feeders.

Fish pirates in dark-painted boats, running without lights, their names and windows blacked out, would creep in under a blanket of fog or the protective covering of a dark night to steal salmon from the fish traps. More than once the sound of gunfire would lace the stillness as some hardy trap watchman fought to protect his silver harvest.

Other pirates, called creek robbers, would slip into the forbidden spawning streams and seine salmon in the act of spawning. Every living thing would get its share of the huge harvest from the sea, and there would still be ample left for spawning.

During the feverish month or six weeks of fishing the canneries and the hundreds of fishermen must make their year's wages. Then, as quickly as it had begun, the season would end.

The traps would be taken from the sea; the canneries' doors would close. One morning all the people and fishing boats that had come north would be gone. Orca City would again be a quiet Alaskan village, its streets empty of all but its regular inhabitants. The bay would have only a few dozen boats left.

The brown bears, rolling fat now, would begin preparing for their winter sleep.

Only Ben would have had none of this harvest. He would have spent all summer chained in the dark interior of the shed, living on an occasional loaf of old stale bread. Ben would not be fat for his winter's sleep.

It was not really warm except directly in the sun. Finally the shadow cast by the eaves of the buildings reached Mark and Ben. A chill breeze came up off the sea and stirred the boy's fine hair. It was neither blond, like his father's, nor black, like his mother's. It was an indefinite in-between brown. His frame was not heavy-boned for thirteen, and there was a delicate look about him. His cheeks were too thin, too white, and his brown eyes were dreamily wistful. They looked too large for his small face.

The bite of the wind finally roused Mark. He started up guiltily. He had to get home. He untied the chain, and said, "Come on, Ben." At the first tug Ben rose and dutifully followed the boy into the dark interior of the shed. Mark retied the chain to the center post exactly as he had found it. Then Ben sniffed at the boy's hands, where the faint aroma of sandwiches still lingered, and his red tongue licked Mark's fingers experimentally.

"I guess you're still hungry," Mark said. He patted Ben's broad head. "I wouldn't have to leave you like this if you were mine. I've got to go now. I'll come again as soon as I can."

Mark gathered up his books and sweater and hurried down the trail toward home. The wind had ruffled the flat surface of the distant bay, and a big fat cloud was bulging into the sky behind the Aleutian Range. It must be a little later than usual, he thought. The sun was poised on top of the mountain.

⚒⚒⚒ 2 ⚒⚒⚒

W HEN Mark's father married Ellen Richards, he had
promised to build her a home anywhere she wanted. She
had chosen a spot above the town so that on one side Orca
City's roofs and the bay lay patterned below them. On the other
the tundra, gently sloping, stretched away to join the distant
mountains. Ellen loved the tundra side because it reminded
her of the rolling acres of her eastern Washington wheat-farm
home. Karl Andersen had built one of Orca City's nicest
homes for his bride. It was a two-story white house sur-
rounded by—a rarity in this northern village—a well-clipped
lawn.

When he opened the door, the first thing Mark saw was his
father standing in the middle of the warm kitchen. He was a
tall wind-tanned man, with a heavy-boned frame and a
straight firm line of mouth and sun-bleached brows. He carried his shoulders squared, his head high. It was topped by
cotton-fine blond hair, and that, too, was bleached lighter by
sun and sea.

For a moment Mark froze, awaiting his father's question.
But his father said, "Well, it's about time! Supper's ready.
Hurry up and wash."

Mark closed the door and ran upstairs to his room to leave
his sweater and books. That was close. He'd have to keep
track of time more carefully after this.

His mother kissed him when he came down, and asked,
"Good day at school?"

"I didn't miss a single homework problem," he said proudly.

"That's fine," she said. But she didn't seem as pleased as he had hoped she would be. "Did you eat all your lunch?"

"I—I left a sandwich in my desk. I forgot it." At least, he thought, it was half true.

"Did you play baseball after school?"

"No." He suddenly felt trapped by his mother's gentle, unaccustomed probing. He fearfully awaited her next question.

But she merely continued to move between stove and table with steaming dishes. As Mark watched her swift, sure movements, he wondered if his mother would ever get old. He bet she wouldn't. His father often said she was just as pretty now as when she came north to teach in Orca City's grade school more than fifteen years ago.

In deference to his mother they ate in the dining room at night. During the meal, which his mother insisted was dinner, not supper, Mark's father told them what had happened in town and along the waterfront. Like every seiner, he was making his own boat, the *Far North*, ready for the coming season.

The *Far North* was 49 feet long and could carry 10,000 salmon in the hold. The crew consisted of Clearwater, an old-time Alaskan, and a third man whom they would pick up from among the new arrivals in town. Karl Andersen had bought the *Far North* four years ago. He had made the final payment on her this spring. The payments had been big. Mark knew that more than once his parents had worried about whether they would be able to make them. His mother had baked a cake in celebration of the last payment, and they had invited Clearwater up for dinner. They had toasted the *Far North*, and his father had waved a fistful of papers and cried: "There she is. She's all ours. That's a load off my back like a ten-ton anchor. Now, maybe, we'll make a little money for a change."

"There's more than two hundred seiners here already," his father was saying. "A couple came in today from 'way down in Mexican waters. They're really tuna clippers temporarily rigged for seining."

His mother asked about their own boat.

"We'll finish overhauling the motor next week," Karl said with satisfaction. "Clearwater'll have the seine patched by tomorrow night. That big sea lion tore it up pretty bad last year when he charged into it."

Mark, half listening, was toying with his food. He was brought up suddenly by a sharp question from his father: "Mark, did you go downtown today and buy some candy?"

Mark looked up, startled. "No, Dad. Why?"

"You're not eating. When I was your age they practically had to nail down the plates."

His mother said anxiously, "Clams rolled in cracker crumbs and fried in butter, Mark. It's one of your favorites."

"I'm just not hungry. Honest, Mother."

His father shook his blond head. "Not natural at your age. You've got to eat more. You're too thin—too—too white. You'll never put on any muscle at this rate," he said in a positive voice.

His mother said gently, "Maybe you'll want something later. Anyway, drink your milk and try to finish that one clam."

There was quiet for a while. Then, into the silence, his father said suddenly, "Fog Benson stopped by today and offered to sell me that bear he's got chained up here in the shed. He wants a hundred dollars."

"Why does he want to sell him?" Ellen asked.

"He needs the money to fix up his boat. He's broke, as

usual. I've also a feeling he's getting afraid of the bear. He can't drag the animal downtown into the bars any more because he's too big. Fog can't handle him, and the bear's too dangerous to be out. So, rather than just shoot him, he'll get a little money out of him if he can. I heard tonight he's trying to sell chances on him, at five dollars a throw. The lucky winner can take the bear out on the tundra, turn him loose, and use him for target practice."

"That's plain brutal!" Ellen said angrily. "The town ought to stop it."

"No one seems much interested. Anyway, Fog's got a problem. Outside a zoo, who wants to buy a bear?"

Mark's heart had begun hammering at his father's first words. The mention of shooting Ben was too much. But he hardly realized he had spoken aloud the thought that flooded his mind until he heard his father's incredulous voice, "Buy the bear for *you? You* want him?"

Mark met his father's startlingly blue eyes and dropped his fork in his confusion.

Karl Andersen leaned across the table, his eyes piercing Mark. "You really mean it? You want Fog Benson's bear? D'you know what you're talking about?"

Mark was afraid to look at his father, whose blue eyes could be as cold as Columbia Glacier. They looked right through you out of that broad, weather-browned face with its long, square jaw.

But since he had gone this far, Mark realized there was nothing for it now but to go on. He raised his eyes briefly to meet his father's intense gaze, then looked at his plate again. "I know. But I—I just want him, Dad," he mumbled miserably.

Karl Andersen studied his small son a moment. He looked

at Mark's mother and said in a curiously quiet voice, "He means it! He really wants that bear! I don't get it!"

His mother circled the table and put her arms around Mark. "Tell your father what happened a few weeks ago."

Mark looked up into his mother's gently smiling face. "Mother, you know?" he asked wonderingly.

"Did you think you could come home late every day with bear hair on your clothes, without my guessing? Now, tell your father."

"Tell me what? What's going on?" his father demanded.

Mark, taking courage within his mother's arms, said in a rush: "I was coming home from school one night, and there was Ben—there was the bear coming right up the trail toward me, dragging his chain. He'd broken the snap and was loose."

"Weren't you frightened?" his mother asked.

"Of Ben?" Mark asked, surprised.

"Go on! Go on!" his father said impatiently.

"I—I took him back to the shed and tied him up," Mark finished lamely.

His father slapped his big hands against his knees and exploded. "Just like that!" he almost shouted. "You'd have me believe you just walked right up to him, picked up the chain, led him back, and tied him up! A five-year-old brownie, half grown, maybe more."

"Well, I petted him some first, and scratched his ears, and rubbed him under the chin. He likes being scratched under the chin."

"Holy mackerel!" his father exclaimed. "Holy mackerel! This is the craziest thing I ever heard of." He looked at Mark's mother accusingly. "You've known this all along?"

"Almost." She combed Mark's straight hair with her fingers.

"Mrs. Miller told me she had seen Mark leading Ben back to the shed the day he got loose."

"You should have told me. Fooling around with a brute like that. Good Lord, Ellen, it's a wonder Mark's alive."

"You and Clearwater were busy working on the boat. Besides, I watched them every day."

"Mother, how could you?" Mark asked. "I never saw you."

"You didn't look in the back of the shed. You just untied Ben every day and sat in the doorway and fed him the lunch you never ate." She looked at her husband. "I was worried the first few times, so I took the rifle with me. Then I began to realize there was really nothing to worry about."

"Nothing to worry about!" his father shouted, shoving his chair back. "Do you know what a brown bear is?"

"Of course," his wife said.

Mark looked at his mother in amazement. There was a soft look about her neat, small-boned body, her shiny black well-kept hair and smooth, lightly tanned face, but there was nothing soft in the way she faced his father. How could she be so calm and sure in the face of his anger?

" 'A brown bear,' " she quoted, " 'is the largest, most dangerous big-game animal in North America. He is the largest carnivorous animal on earth. He is the last living relic of those fabulous hairy mammals of the Ice Age who migrated from Asia and Russia millions of years ago—such as the giant sloth and the saber-toothed tiger. He is a direct descendant of the legendary Siberian cave bear.' "

"Very good," his father said with heavy sarcasm. "But you left out that he also happens to be the most unpredictable animal on earth."

"That's local gossip."

"It's the opinion of everyone who's ever come up against 'em. What's wrong with you, Ellen? You've lived here fifteen years. You know better. And you're his mother. Don't you understand the danger in this at all?"

His mother's face became grave. She said to Mark, "If you're through eating, why don't you run up to your room and do your homework now?"

Mark could have told her that this was Friday night and that he never did homework before Saturday night. But the anger between his parents, and his father's explosive temper, frightened him. He was glad to get away. He slipped off his chair without glancing at his father, ran from the room and up the stairs. He leaned against the closed door, his whole body shaking, his heart pounding. How had it happened so fast? One moment everything had been fine, his mother and father smiling and happy, the feeling of family closeness a warmth in the room. The next moment there was his father's angry, accusing voice.

What he had said about wanting Ben had caused this, of course. If only it hadn't slipped out. But in a way he was glad it had. The fear of being found out was over at last. He hadn't dreamed his father would be so angry. They would be talking about him and Ben down there now. He wished he could know what they were saying. He thought of the register in the hall floor. His father had installed it several years ago so the heat from downstairs could come up to warm the second floor in the winter.

He eased the door open, crept down the hall, and stretched out on his stomach by the metal grille. The dining table was directly below. His father's cotton-blond head was on one side and his mother's smooth dark one on the other. He could hear their voices plainly.

His mother was saying in a quiet, serious voice, "There's something I haven't told you, Karl."

"I'll say there is!" his father said.

"I'm not talking about a tame bear."

His father didn't answer for a moment, but when he did the anger was gone from his voice. "All right," he asked. "What is it?"

Mark could see his mother's slender hands twisted together before her on the tabletop. "Remember how it was with Jamie?"

"How could I forget?" his father said gently. He stretched a long arm across the table and covered her clenched hands with his big brown one. "That's why I don't want Mark fooling around with this bear. He's all we've got left."

His mother's voice sounded hurt and frightened: "He's too thin. He—he doesn't eat well. He just sits about and does nothing. He has no vitality. And he's so white."

"He's just taken a spurt of growth," his father soothed. "All boys go through it."

"We said that about Jamie, and it wasn't true."

"What are you trying to tell me?"

"I took Mark to Dr. Walker for his checkup. He says Mark shows every indication of being ripe for the same trouble Jamie had."

"Tuberculosis!" His father reared back in his chair angrily. "I don't believe it! Walker's not perfect. He can be wrong! He's always hanging crepe! The boy's just taken a spurt of growth, I tell you." He was almost yelling. "Can't Walker say something hopeful and cheerful, just once?"

"He said 'there were indications,'" Mark's mother said patiently. "Mark was exposed, you know. But Mark doesn't have it now. If we can build him up so he has some resistance, he'll be all right. We didn't have that chance with Jamie."

Mark dismissed the talk about himself. The important thing was what they might say about Ben.

His father was speaking again. "All right. What does he need?"

"Lots of exercise—outdoor exercise to toughen him up, to stimulate his appetite; good wholesome food, and plenty of rest."

"That's easy enough."

"It's very hard," his mother said. "Just stop and think. Who does Mark have to play with? This is a small school. The children his size are younger and several grades lower. He has nothing in common with them. Those his own age and in his grade are bigger and stronger. He's not capable of playing with them. He doesn't want to play. He'd rather stay in and read or just lie around and do nothing."

"Drive him out," his father said. "Sometimes you have to make kids do things."

His mother shook her dark head. "I do drive him out, but I can't make him play, and what would he play at alone? He needs an interest or something that will challenge him. Lately he's found an interest."

"That bear?"

Mark held his breath, waiting.

"If he needs a pet," his father said, "we'll get him a dog."

"It's too late," his mother's voice answered. "Mark's given his heart to Ben."

"That's nonsense."

"I knew a little girl in the States who had a full-grown lion for a pet," his mother went on calmly. "It went to the school bus with her in the morning and waited beside the road for her at night. She could have had a dog or a horse, but she loved the lion."

"There's no sense to that kind of argument," his father said emphatically. "The whole idea is—is preposterous."

"You once told me you had a pet seal. You must have seen thousands of baby seals and dogs up here. Why a baby seal, Karl? And why that one? Do you remember how it was?"

Mark didn't know his father had ever had a pet. He brought his ear closer to the register so as not to miss a word.

"Sure, I remember," his father said. "He was a little fellow sunning himself on a log. I rowed the boat toward him, and he just lay there and watched me, his eyes big and round and unafraid. We looked at each other, and suddenly I wanted him more than I'd ever wanted anything in my life. My dad argued and tried to reason with me, but it was no use. Finally he let me keep the seal. I had him until he weighed over a hundred pounds and was a nuisance to everybody. A drunken fisherman eventually killed him."

So his father had had a seal for a pet when he was a boy. Then he must understand how it is with Ben and me, Mark thought, his heart beginning to hammer.

"Why didn't you choose a dog or even some other animal?" Mark heard his mother ask.

"I don't know," Karl answered. "It just had to be that particular seal."

"I had a baby coyote," Mark's mother said. "Why I picked up that mangy little scrub on the prairie when we had a whole farm full of domestic animals I could love, I don't know. I only know that sometimes something does happen between people and animals. There seems to be a bond that overcomes all fear, prejudice, everything objectionable. I suppose you might call it a perfect love, a sort of Biblical 'lion and the lamb' kind of love. It happened to me and my little coyote. It was the most wonderful thing in the world to me at that time. It happened with you and your seal, too, didn't it?"

"A lot of fishermen pick up baby seals and keep 'em a few weeks," his father argued. "They're cute."

"That's not why you picked up yours."

"This kind of talk is crazy, Ellen. A baby seal is no brown bear."

"What I'm saying," she said patiently, "is that the same wonderful thing that happened to us and our pets has happened to Mark and Ben. That's why I'm not afraid."

It came to Mark with a shock that his mother was actually arguing with his father for him and Ben. She was standing up against his father. She looked as soft as a young girl, with her pliant body, her slender, smooth hands, her small head crowned by its neat wealth of shining black hair. But she was not soft. As his father had once said, "Underneath, Ellen's tough as whalebone." If she could stand against his father . . . Maybe, Mark thought wildly, oh, maybe . . .

"How can you be sure?" his father's voice asked.

"I've watched them together for two weeks."

"Okay," his father's voice bored in again, "for the sake of argument let's suppose you're right. Do you know what would happen if Ben turned ugly for one second and took a swipe at Mark with his paw?"

"I've thought of that possibility," his mother said calmly. "But I keep asking myself, knowing what I do now . . . if we'd had this chance to save Jamie, would I have taken it? I would."

"You're willing to risk Mark's life with Ben on some—some vague feeling that those two understand each other and nothing will happen?"

"It's not just a feeling and it's not vague," she said positively. "I know. I also know how wild this idea seems. At first it sent me into a panic when I thought of it. It took days to get used to the thought. But we have to do something and we have to do it now. If we were in a big city down in the States, there'd be all sorts of measures we could take. But we aren't. We're in the Territory of Alaska, two thousand miles from the nearest large city. We have to make do with what we have."

"How would owning a bear help?"

"Mark wants him very much. Ben can be the incentive that drives him out to work. Lots of outdoor exercise, Dr. Walker said. He'll have to exercise plenty for Ben's keep. He'll have to cut and dry grass for bedding, see the shed is kept clean. He'd have to earn the fish Ben eats and whatever else he gives him. Don't you see, we could add as many requirements as we think necessary to help build up Mark's health."

I could do those things easy, Mark thought, his hopes soaring with his mother's arguments. I could do a lot more than that.

His father said, "You've got it all figured out, haven't you? You're sure we're not just blowing up a storm of worry because of what happened to Jamie?"

"Jamie made me aware of the danger signals. I see those signals in Mark. Don't you see them, too?"

His father nodded. "I guess I just haven't wanted to admit it." He rose, walked around the table, and put his hands on Ellen's shoulders. His voice was gentle. "This is the craziest idea I've ever heard. The way you explain it, it sounds reasonable. But it's not, Ellen. Not with a brown bear. I've known of at least two men who were badly mauled by them and I saw one that had been killed. It wasn't a pretty sight."

"People have been badly mauled by dogs, too," she said. "But that hasn't condemned all dogs."

"Perhaps I'm prejudiced. But to me it's a little like jumping off a burning ship and not being able to swim."

"Not in this case," she said promptly.

"Maybe if I'd had as long to get used to the idea as you've had, it would have made a difference in my thinking. But this, Ellen . . ." He dropped his hands and turned toward the coat closet. "I'm willing to do almost anything. And we will do something. We'll talk about this again tomorrow. I've got to go down to the boat for a while."

"Karl," Mark's mother did not turn her head, "do you really think time will change your mind?"

Mark could hear his father shrugging into his coat. "No," he finally said, "not at all." He went out, closing the door firmly behind him.

Mark edged back from the register, carefully tiptoed to his room, and closed the door. His hopes, so high a moment ago, were destroyed. He could tell by his father's tone of voice and the way he had closed the door, that he would never change his mind. His dream of someday owning Ben was gone forever. In fact—he faced it now for the first time—it had always been just a dream. He should have known it could never come true. Tomorrow, or the day after, Ben would be taken out and shot by some sportsman whose five-dollar chance had won him the right to shoot a trusting bear.

3

MARK ran across the tundra crying, "Ben, Ben!" He saw the man carrying the rifle and leading Ben out on the tundra. For a moment he didn't understand. Ben walked beside the man like a well-trained dog on a leash. Finally the man stopped and unhooked the chain from about Ben's neck. He stepped back, half raised the rifle to his shoulder, and waited.

Then Mark knew. He began to run.

Ben looked at the man. He swung his big head and looked all about. The man yelled. He waved his arms and made threatening gestures with the gun. Finally Ben started walking away, head down, sniffing the fresh tundra moss as he went. The man let him get a few feet off, then calmly raised the rifle, and shot. Ben collapsed.

Mark screamed, "Ben! Ben!"

Ben raised himself, turned his head, and looked at the man. Mark was so close he could see the surprise on Ben's broad face. Then the bear began digging frantically into the tundra with his forepaws as he tried to drag his broken, paralyzed hindquarters away. The man shot him again.

Mark cried brokenly, "Ben! Ben!" He was running through the soft, yielding tundra.

He awoke sobbing. It took several minutes to realize it had been a dream.

But this terrible thing was going to happen; perhaps it had already! Mark crawled out of bed and went to the window to see. It would likely take place right out there, within sight of the house.

From his upstairs window the full sweep of the tundra was spread before Mark. He could see the edge where it fell away to the lowland where the creek flowed and the waist-high grass grew. Beyond that, the white line of the mountains reared.

It was early. The sun was only a couple of hours high. It lay bright and shining across the tundra, making it look as smooth and soft as velvet. It bathed the distant mountains until they glittered like white upside-down ice-cream cones.

Mark searched the tundra anxiously. There was no man, no brown hump that could be a dead bear. It hadn't happened yet. But Fog Benson would have no trouble selling chances. A lot of men were anxious to shoot any kind of bear. "Dead game sports" his father called them. He might see Ben killed, or maybe he would hear the shot.

It would be just as bad to hear the shot, because then he would see it all in his mind. He wished there was someplace he could go until it was over.

It was very early, but Mark was no longer sleepy.

As he dressed slowly, he sought for a way to save Ben.

He was sitting on the edge of the bed pulling on his shoe when, like a parka squirrel popping into a hole, a thought popped into his mind. Maybe Ben had got loose during the night and wandered away. Mark thought about that hopeful possibility. Ben had broken the snap on his chain once and got loose. Maybe he could do it again.

The more he thought of it, the more he hoped Ben had got away. If he was loose, he could head for those distant white mountains, and no hunter would ever find him.

Mark knew his father and mother would not be up for another hour. There was time to slip up to the shed, and see. He finished dressing quickly, eased his door open, crept silently

33

down the stairs and out the back door. He rounded the side of the house and hurried up the trail.

But the moment he entered the shed's dark interior and called to the bear in a guarded voice, he heard the rattle of Ben's chain. His heart sank.

The big body brushed against him, and Ben's damp nose began pushing and sniffing at his hands for food. Mark put his arms around Ben's neck and said, "Why didn't you get away last night? Oh, Ben, why didn't you?"

He untied the chain and moved it to the outside post so that Ben could stand in the doorway and feel the early-morning sunlight and snuff the crisp air. Mark stood beside him, a hand on the broad head, absently rubbing the base of the tulip-shaped ears, and thinking. At any minute the man who had won the right to kill Ben might come up the trail. He thought of his dream. It had been so real. That's just how it will be, he thought. If only I hadn't brought Ben back the day I found him loose. If I'd just taken the broken chain off and let him go, no one would ever have known. It's my fault Ben is going to be killed. I owe him something for that.

Then another thought entered his mind: If I turn Ben loose now, it would be almost the same as if I hadn't brought him back that first time.

The thought was so shocking that at first his mind refused to accept it. But the more he thought about it, the more logical it became.

It wouldn't take long to hike with Ben across the tundra to that depression where it dropped away to the small valley and the creek. There he could turn Ben loose, and the bear would have a chance to escape. It would be easy to return and tie the chain to the post again. No one would ever know Ben hadn't escaped again.

Mark untied the chain. For a moment he stood there, trying not to think of the consequences if he were caught, but his heart was pounding and his legs were weak. If his father ever learned of this, or Fog Benson or anybody— He put his fear resolutely behind him. This was for Ben. He was saving Ben's life. "Come on." He pulled on the chain. For a frantic instant he half hoped Ben would refuse to follow. But the bear dropped dutifully to follow at his heels. Then Mark knew he was committed to the act, and he stepped fearfully out on the tundra.

This was the most dangerous part. They would be in the open until they disappeared over the rim of that small valley.

He tried to hurry Ben, but the feel of the tundra beneath the bear's feet was new. He wanted to stop and sniff and blow in the fine moss or scratch at it with a paw.

"Come on, come on." Mark jerked on the chain. "I'm trying to save your life. If someone sees us, you'll be killed. Come on, Ben!" He coaxed Ben into a trot, but their progress was agonizingly slow. At every step Mark expected a warning shout behind them.

They finally reached the rim of the valley and dipped down into the lowland where the stream was. It was not marshy here. There was no waist-high grass. That grew beyond the near bend. But they were out of sight, and it was safe to turn Ben loose.

Mark knelt before him, gripping the chain on either side of the big neck to hold the furry head still. Ben thrust his wet nose against Mark's face, and snuffled loudly. Mark began to speak in a low tone, slowly, carefully, as though in this way Ben could understand.

"I wish I could keep you, but I can't. We could have lots of fun if you were mine. But nobody thinks you can have fun being friends with a bear, especially a brown bear like you.

That's because they don't know you like I do. They think the only fun you can have with bears is shooting them. That's why I brought you out here. You have to go away. Go far away, up in the mountains where they can never find you. And stay there, you understand? Don't ever come back. I don't want you to be killed. You'll find lots of other bears up there. And you won't be chained up in an old shed anymore, or have to eat stale bread and things like that. You'll be happy. And you'll be free." He put his cheek against Ben's broad forehead, and murmured, "I won't ever see you again, Ben."

He scratched the base of Ben's tulip ears a last time, and the bear rolled his big head so that Mark could scratch first one ear and then the other. He rubbed the fur under his chin, and Ben closed his eyes, stretched his neck out, and grunted happily.

Mark rose suddenly, unsnapped the chain, and said in a rush, "You're free now. Good-bye, Ben. Good-bye!"

He pushed Ben's head aside, turned hurriedly, and began climbing back up the slope. Because it was hard to see where he was going, he slipped once, and fell.

Before he reached the top he heard a sound, and there was Ben, padding at his heels as contentedly as if still fastened to the chain. Mark waved his arms. He yelled: "Go away! You're free. Can't you understand that? Get out of here. Quit following me!"

Ben came up to him and shoved his nose against Mark's hands. Mark pushed his head away. "You want them to find you? You want to be killed? Get away from me!" He struck Ben between the eyes with his fist. Ben continued to push and sniff at him. He struck again, blindly, forgetting he held the chain in his hand. The links slashed cruelly across Ben's tender nose.

36

Ben reared back, and Mark saw the same hurt, surprised look he'd seen in his dream when the man had shot him. Mark put his arms around Ben's neck, buried his face in his fur, and began to cry. "Go away," he sobbed. "Please go away, Ben."

Ben was as immovable as stone.

Mark began to realize that if he was going to save Ben he would have to lead him away, then try to sneak off when Ben was not looking. He turned and ran back downhill toward the bottom land, and Ben padded happily at his heels.

At the bottom, Mark turned up the valley toward the bend where the long sedge grass grew. Once Ben got interested in eating, it would be easy to sneak around the bend and out of sight. Ben would go on eating and eventually wander away.

The moment they rounded the bend, they were in grass almost shoulder-high to Ben. He plunged into it and began tearing out huge mouthfuls, his big jaws chewing as fast as they could. It was the first he had ever tasted, and he was ravenous.

Mark glanced toward the rim of the valley. He could relax a little before sneaking off. Anyone seeking them would have to come right into the valley to see them. He didn't have to worry about getting home for a while yet. He sat down on a clump of grass and folded his arms over his knees.

He was conscious of the feeling of wildness and of being utterly alone in a huge and vacant land. The stream was about a hundred feet away, clear, shallow, and ice cold from the melting glaciers that fed it. Soon it would be boiling with salmon.

Mark remembered when he and Jamie had come down here several years ago to see the salmon spawn. They had lain on their stomachs on the creekbank and watched a mother salmon fan her tail against the bottom and dig a small hole in which she had deposited eight or nine hundred eggs. A male salmon had swum over the spot, and a milky substance had floated down to fertilize the eggs. Other salmon were doing the same thing all along the bottom. Afterward they would cruise back and forth over the eggs until the salmon turned red, then white, and finally died. They really rotted to death, Clearwater said. In time the eggs would hatch, and the baby salmon, called fingerlings, would swim down the creek and out to sea. "No one knows where the fingerlings go," Clearwater had said. "Maybe clear around the world. In three years they'll come back, fully grown salmon. They'll swim up this creek and lay their eggs on this very spot, most likely, and then they, too, will die."

A pair of blue jays set up a racket on a bush behind Mark. An eagle planed out of the cloudless sky and landed on a snag. His sharp eyes were on the creek, looking for salmon. There was a steady *rip-rip* as Ben tore into the grass clumps. Mark became fascinated as he watched the huge jaws snip off the clumps. Ben reared on his hind legs several times and looked about, chewing blissfully. Mark laughed outright. Ben reminded him of some old hairy-coated prospector who hadn't shaved for weeks.

The eagle screamed with angry disappointment, and flapped away. The blue jays continued their noisy conversation. Ben's stomach began to bulge. He was selecting the grass clumps he ate more carefully now. He sniffed and blew noisily into each clump, choosing only the tenderest shoots.

Ben had not wandered off in his eating, as Mark had thought he would. The growth was so lush he had eaten his fill within a short distance. Mark had had no chance to sneak away.

Farther on, the grass ended at a boulder field. If he could get Ben interested in the grubs and mice under the rocks, he would have to wander in his search for more, and perhaps Mark could get away.

He snapped the chain around Ben's neck, and Ben, his craving for grass temporarily filled, followed willingly.

At the boulder field Ben immediately began sniffing at a half buried rock. Mark pried up the rock. Under it were a half dozen long white grubs. Ben's red tongue shot out; the grubs disappeared, and Ben stood licking his lips.

Mark turned over another rock and found more grubs. Ben's nose was down, waiting at the next boulder. But Mark could not turn it over. He felt along the sides for a handhold. Ben became impatient, and pawed at the rock. His big claws caught at the edge and ripped it out of the earth. There were more grubs, and a pair of mice darted out. Ben's big paw struck with lightning speed. Both mice and grubs disappeared. Ben lumbered to the next rock.

Mark worked on half a dozen more rocks before Ben got the idea and began turning them over alone.

Mark sat down and leaned against a boulder. He'd wait until Ben wandered away; then he could sneak off. The rock was warm against his back. The jays had disappeared, and complete silence had closed over the valley. Not a breath of air stirred the leaves of the nearby alders. He was so tired his muscles jumped. He glanced up at the sun. He couldn't stay away much longer.

4

ELLEN Andersen made little noise as she hurried about the cheerful, sunlit kitchen getting breakfast. She didn't want to wake Mark. On Saturdays she let him sleep late. The extra rest was good for him.

Karl came into the kitchen. He stood looking thoughtfully out the window, legs stiff and braced apart, head thrown back with an almost arrogant air. His blond hair, glistening with water, made an odd contrast with his tanned skin.

Let that blond hair grow; give him a spear and shield, and you've got a Viking right out of the history books, Ellen thought.

They ate at the small breakfast table. Karl poured a generous helping of syrup over his pancakes, and said, "Can't get Mark and that bear out of my head. A thirteen-year-old kid with a brown bear for a pet." He shook his head. "You know what would happen down in the States if we tried a stunt like this? The authorities would land on us like a ton of bricks." He waved his fork. "Cruelty to kids—or animals—or something. They wouldn't tolerate it a second."

"I guess it wasn't a very good idea," Ellen agreed quietly. "But I was willing to try anything."

"I know." Karl finished his pancakes, drank his coffee, and glanced at the clock. "Mark ought to be getting up soon. Think I'll roust him out. Want to talk with him before I leave."

"Don't be rough with him," Ellen said anxiously. "It's bad enough that he can't have Ben."

40

"I won't torture him," Karl said stiffly. "I want to talk with him, that's all."

He disappeared up the stairs, and Ellen heard him enter Mark's room. Moments later he was back. "Mark's gone! Where would he take off to this early?"

Ellen glanced at the clock. There was only one place. She said, "Go up and look in the shed where Ben is."

"He knows better than to go up there, especially after last night."

"He knew better before last night. Go look in the shed."

Karl pulled on his coat, grumbling. "Kids! Sometimes I wonder if they're worth the trouble." He scooped up the rifle from behind the door and a handful of shells from the shelf. He strode out, stuffing shells into the magazine.

"Be easy with him," Ellen warned from the doorway.

Karl didn't answer.

Ellen watched him swing up the trail and into the shed. He was gone only a moment, and emerged again. He bent and studied the ground, then rose and began walking with long strides straight out across the tundra toward the valley where the land dipped down to the creek.

It's just what I would have done, Ellen thought. Oh, Mark. I'm so sorry!

The trail was easy for Andersen to follow. Ben's big feet had sunk into the soft tundra moss at every step. It led to the break, down into the valley, and turned upcreek into the sedge. He saw where Ben had eaten. The trail through the sedge was three feet wide.

Andersen found them in the boulder field beyond. He stepped from the high grass, and there they were, not twenty feet in front of him. He pulled up short, the gun halfway to his shoulder. Mark and Ben's friendship had prepared him for something unusual. But not this.

"Holy mackerel!" he gasped under his breath. "Will you look at that!"

Because he was downwind from them, Ben hadn't got his scent, and the marshy land had muffled Karl's steps. He stood perfectly still for some seconds, telling himself he was really seeing what he thought he was seeing. "That's Mark lying there beside a brownie. My Mark!" He moved cautiously forward for a better look. He held the rifle ready across his chest. His fingers ached with the pressure of his convulsive grip. The rifle was his reassurance, his and Mark's protection if the bear suddenly became excited.

He was fooling himself. The rifle was no protection. He wouldn't dare use it with Mark there so close; besides, he would never have time. That brute could strike and kill with the speed of light.

Mark half lay, his shoulders propped against a rock, sound asleep. His small thin face was grimy and tear-streaked. His hands were dirty; the knees of his pants were caked with mud. Ben was stretched out beside him, his big head flat on outstretched forepaws. One paw with its long, cruelly studded claws, was actually resting against Mark's leg. Mark's arm lay along Ben's neck, fingers buried in the coarse fur. Andersen hadn't seen the bear in months. He was obviously underfed, but his frame was big and solid. The evidence of their activity lay all about in a mass of overturned rocks. From his appearance Mark had turned rocks, too, until he was worn out. The bear, typical of all bears with a full stomach, wanted a nap.

Just like a boy and his dog. How had Ellen put it last night? Something about a love that overcame fear and suspicion. A sort of Biblical "lion and lamb" kind of love—he remembered that part. Last night it had sounded farfetched, melodramatic. But not now, he thought. Not now, when I'm standing here looking at this.

Ben's eyes opened. The big head rose, and Ben looked directly at him. Karl stepped back involuntarily. But Ben just lay there, his small eyes fastened on Andersen with as direct a look as he'd ever encountered. He seemed to be frowning, annoyed at this intrusion. Then, as Karl continued to stare at him, he realized it was the way Ben's eyes were set deep in his fur, under the heavy shelf of forehead bone, that created this impression. There was no frown, nor was there anger or fear in Ben's eyes. His look seemed to be one of almost human curiosity.

Andersen wet his dry lips. Making his voice as quiet, as completely toneless as possible, he called, "Mark. Mark. Wake up."

Mark opened his eyes, blinking at the bright sunlight. Then he saw his father with a rifle. He started up, crying, "No! No! Dad. Please don't!"

"Calm down," Andersen said in the same quiet, toneless voice. "I came for you."

Mark's excited voice had brought Ben to his feet. Mark clung to his neck with both hands. Ben ignored Andersen, and swung his big head around to snuffle loudly at the boy's face.

Andersen said, "You brought Ben out here to turn him loose?"

"I can't let them kill him, Dad. I can't."

"What happens to Ben is no concern of yours."

"But it's not right to shoot him," Mark cried. "He hasn't done anything."

"It's not right for you to interfere in other people's business either," Andersen said sternly.

43

"But, Dad——"

"You stole him, Mark."

"I was only trying to save him."

"That's no excuse. If you'd stayed away from him in the beginning, you wouldn't be in this mess."

"I didn't want to keep going to see him. I tried to stay away," Mark said miserably. "But he was lonesome and always in the dark, and with hardly anything to eat. And now just because old Fog Benson doesn't want him any more, he's going to let somebody shoot him for five dollars."

Andersen lowered himself carefully to a rock, never taking his eyes off Ben. He said kindly: "I don't like it either, Mark. I'd like to turn Ben loose and let him go back up in the mountains with other brownies where he belongs. But we can't just take things into our own hands because we've decided they're wrong. We have to live by the rules, even when those rules don't always seem right. And the rule here is that Ben belongs to Fog Benson. He has a right to do with him as he likes, and we don't."

"Even selling chances to kill a tame bear?" Mark asked.

"Even that. Things don't always turn out the way we'd like them to, Mark. Now you're going to take Ben back where you got him."

"But they'll kill him, Dad."

Andersen stood up. "We're not going to discuss this any further. You know the right thing to do, Mark. Put the chain on him. Now!"

There was no arguing with the flat command in his father's voice. Mark fumbled blindly with the chain and snapped it around Ben's neck.

At the shed his father gave him just time to tie Ben to the center post, then took his arm and led him out and down the trail toward home. He didn't have a chance to say good-bye to Ben, or even to take a last look. His father was going to punish him. He knew that set of his mouth and chin. But he didn't care. Nothing mattered now. Ben would be killed.

The moment they came through the door, his mother had her arms around him. "Mark!" she said, "Oh, Mark." She held him off at arm's length and looked at him. "You go right upstairs and wash and change clothes. When you come down I'll have your breakfast ready."

"I'm not hungry," he mumbled.

His father said sharply, "Do as your mother says! And don't be all day about it."

It took only a couple of minutes to wash and change clothes. When he returned, his father sat at the table with two sheets of paper before him. He motioned Mark to a chair and said, "Last night you wanted me to buy Ben, and I said 'No.' There was more to that 'No' than just the fact that a brown bear is a dangerous animal and not exactly my idea of a fit playmate. You're old enough to understand those other reasons for my refusal. All you've thought of is that you want Ben for a pet. There's more to it than that. Pets are expensive to keep, and Ben, in particular, would be. Last night I figured out what it would cost to buy and support Ben. It's all here on this page," his father said, pushing a sheet of paper toward him. "I want you to take a good look at it.

"I've written down $100. That's the price Fog Benson's asking for Ben. There's $50 for that old shed to keep him in. There's the cost of feed, old bread, and such things. You'll get it cheap at stores and restaurants, but you'll still have to pay something. Another $100. During the salmon season he should have fish. I get $0.40 a fish from the cannery, so every fish Ben eats is $0.40. That right?"

45

"I—I thought I could take him down to the creek and let him catch his own salmon," Mark said.

"Can't count on that. You'll see why in a minute. Ben will eat ten or twelve fish a day. Call it ten. That's $4 a day. A 45-day season makes it $180. All that adds up to $430 for Ben in one year."

"I didn't think of all that," Mark said weakly.

"That's not all of it," his father pursued. "The shed needs a new roof and a window for light. It should be fixed better inside for his winter sleep. That's more money. We haven't a whole lot of cash on hand right now. You know that."

Yes, he knew. He'd heard his father and mother talking, planning night after night before they finished the payments on the *Far North*. She was an expensive boat, and they had saved a long time for her.

His father shoved the other paper across. "Now let's look at this one. Owning an animal like Ben wouldn't be just stopping at night after school to play with him. You'd have responsibilities. I've written some of them down there. Cut and dry grass for bedding. Clean the shed every day and keep it clean. Scrounge around and get his food, the old bread and such."

"I could do that," Mark insisted.

"There's more, and it's not so easy." His father leaned back and spoke in a man-to-man voice: "I hire two men aboard the boat during the season, you know. One is Clearwater, the other a pickup. You could help pay back that $480 I'd be spending by taking the place of the pickup."

"Are you sure he could take a man's place?" Mark's mother asked anxiously.

"He could keep the seine neatly piled, the boat clean, ride on top of the wheelhouse, and spot for schools of salmon. He could even take a turn at the wheel in open water."

"Oh, I could, Dad. I know I could!" Mark said eagerly.

"You'd be aboard all season," his father continued. "Home Sundays and a few hours the days we came in with a load of fish. Your mother would be alone here. And who'd feed Ben while you were on the boat?"

Mark hadn't thought of that. The hope that had begun to build within him oozed away.

His mother said quietly, "I'm not afraid of being alone while my men are out working. And I'll feed Ben." She smiled at Karl. "I've petted him a number of times. We get along very well."

Mark was on his feet. Color had rushed into his pale cheeks. "Dad, would you, then?" His voice was climbing with sudden hope.

"Sit down," his father said firmly. "I'm not through."

Mark sat down.

His father said, "You know, I never take anyone aboard the boat who can't swim."

"I'll learn," Mark promised. "It won't take me long."

"You didn't learn last summer or the summer before."

"I—I didn't really try—not awfully hard. But I can. I know I can, Dad."

"Read that second page over carefully," his father said. "Are you sure you could do all those things and do them on time?"

Mark scarcely heard his father and he didn't see the writing on the paper at all. All he saw was Ben. "I could do it!" he insisted. "I could do it easy."

His father's bright blue eyes studied him. "All right," he agreed finally. "Take that sheet upstairs and tack it on the wall over your bed. I'll buy Ben for you."

"Dad! You mean it—you'll buy him? You'll buy Ben? You really will?"

"I really will," his father said, and for the first time that morning Karl Andersen smiled.

Mark shot out of the chair. The chair crashed over. "Wow!" he shouted. "Ben! Ben, oh, Ben. You're mine! Mine! All mine!"

He waved the paper frantically and danced around the room. He charged around the table and kissed his mother. "He's mine! Ben's mine! Nobody can kill him now." He stopped short and looked at his father. "That's part of the rule, isn't it, Dad? Nobody can kill Ben now?"

"That's right," his father said. "The rule's on your side now."

"On my side! Oh, on my side!" Mark chanted. He rushed around the table and, for one of the few times in his life, threw his arms around his father and kissed him with wild abandon.

His father said, "The chair, Mark! Pick up the chair."

He dived at the chair, jerked it upright, and shoved it in the general direction of the table. It hit the table with a bang and crashed over sideways. By that time Mark was halfway to the stairs, waving the paper and yelling at the top of his lungs, "Wow! Wow! Mine, all mine! On my side now!" He made a flying leap for the third step, missed, and landed halfway on the bottom step. He sprawled and rolled on the floor. Before his mother could start from her chair and go to him, he was charging up the stairs, thin legs flying, arms flailing.

It took only a few seconds to find a couple of pins and tack the instructions to the wall. He was just finishing when a frightening thought occurred to him. It sent him pounding frantically back down the stairs, shouting, "Dad! Dad! maybe Fog Benson has sold Ben. Maybe he's gone."

"No, he isn't," his father said calmly. "I hunted up Fog last night and made a deal with him. He's to hold Ben until noon for me. I needed time to think this over."

"You can still buy Ben if you pay Fog by this noon?" Mark persisted.

"That's right. We have plenty of time."

Mark's mother said: "So you inspected the shed last night in the dark. And made out those two lists. I wondered what kept you up so late. Why didn't you tell Mark when you found him with Ben this morning that you had a deal pending with Benson?"

"I wanted Mark to realize he'd saved Ben by agreeing to all the conditions on that paper. I think he realizes it now."

"No wonder everyone loves the Danes." Mark's mother smiled. "They're an awfully smart people."

"Remember that, next time you're tempted to start throwing crockery," Karl told her.

"Can we go see Ben right away?" Mark asked. "I've got to tell him. I've got to take him out in the sun. Can we go right now, Dad?"

"All right." His father reached behind the door for the rifle. He held it a moment, his dark face thoughtful. Then he dropped it into the crook of his arm. "Let's go," he said.

They went up the path together, and Mark could not help noticing how his father's broad shoulders were back, his head high, the crest of blond hair shining in the bright morning sun. Mark danced about his father excitedly, pouring out a stream of talk and waving his arms. His father finally said, "You haven't shown this much life in a year. Maybe buying Ben isn't such a bad idea." Then he added in a low voice, as though talking to himself, "I hope it isn't. I sure hope to God it isn't!"

5

T HE days following the purchase of Ben were a busy time for everyone.

Spring was charging full tilt toward the short northern summer with its maximum twenty hours of daylight. Fish traps were set at sea with watchmen already on board. Crews had checked into the canneries where every machine was ready and waiting. Every living thing whose roots were anchored in the rich northern arth was growing with wild abandon. And somewhere at sea countless millions of salmon were bearing down on the Alaskan coast; returning with mystifying accuracy to the very streams where they had been spawned three years before. The opening of the salmon season was but days away.

The bay at the foot of town was now packed with seiners of every shape, size, and color, "One thousand and one hundred by actual count," Karl Andersen said one day. Orca City's one mud street and old wooden sidewalks were jammed night and day with milling fishermen impatiently awaiting opening day.

Andersen and Clearwater had completed overhauling the *Far North,* and she lay at her berth, waiting. The last job had been the dipping of the 900-foot seine into the brine tank so that the salt action of the sea would not eat it away. Now it was a beautiful sky-blue bundle piled neatly on the turntable in the stern.

Mark had been as busy as anyone these past days. As his father had predicted, owning Ben had created a great amount of work. There was no time now to sit in the warm spring sun, his head against Ben's solid side, dreaming what he would do if Ben were his. Ben *was* his, and the responsibility was a full-time job.

The first thing he had done was to visit both grocery stores in town, where he tried to bargain for their old bread. But with all the seasonal people pouring into Orca City, there was no old bread. He had better luck at the three restaurants. They gave him all the scraps simply for hauling them away. Every other day he took the wheelbarrow down the hill to town and hauled the five-gallon cans of scraps up to Ben's shed. Every night he had to change Ben's bed, put in new straw, and fill his water and feed bowls.

Mark enjoyed working around Ben. He could watch him eat and listen to the satisfied smacking of his lips as he dug into the piles of food. And Ben ate an amazing quantity. Mark could almost see him gaining weight. The sharp ridge of his backbone was disappearing with the added pounds, and the hard cage of his ribs was now padded with flesh. He had shed most of his rough winter coat, rubbing it off against the big center post. His summer coat was emerging a shiny golden-taffy brown.

Only one thing marred Mark's complete happiness with Ben. His father was always present. Karl Andersen had laid down hard and fast rules. Mark was not to bring any of his school friends around. Half the school had followed him home that first night. His mother had seen them from the kitchen window and shooed them away. Even so, she had been visited by several worried mothers. What she had told them Mark never knew, but no children followed him again. He was not to go into the shed and work around close to Ben unless his father was there. And each day he was there, sitting in the open doorway, the rifle across his knees, eyes sharp for any unfriendly move Ben might make.

For the first few days his father was always warning Mark, his voice sharp and annoyed: "Don't get so close to him. Shove that food dish to him with a stick. Don't carry the hay up to him for his bedding. Shove it in with the pitchfork. That's what pitchforks are for. And for Pete's sake don't get so close to his head. Perhaps he looks tame, and right now he acts tame. But he's not. He's a wild animal. He's a brownie. And don't you ever forget it."

Mark felt that his father was being unreasonable, but he never complained. His father simply didn't know Ben. The important thing was that Ben had not been killed. He was his, and Mark was glad to have him under any conditions.

But it was hard to remember to stay at arm's length from Ben. He wanted to scratch Ben under the chin until he stretched his big neck out flat and closed his eyes with pleasure. He wanted to rub his ears and watch the big head roll so that he scratched first one ear and then the other. He knew that Ben expected attention, and could not understand why he no longer got it.

Day after day his father sat in the doorway with the rifle, and Mark was sure he suspected none of this.

After several days, during which nothing happened, his father began to relax. The rifle lay loosely across his knees, and he spent much of the time looking out over the town's roofs and down toward the distant bay where row on row of boats awaited the opening of the salmon season.

It was during one of these long looks that Mark ran his hand around the inside of Ben's feed bowl and was letting Ben lick the particles of food off his extended fingers when his father's voice said sharply, "Mark! get away from him. How many times have I told you not to get so close?"

"But, Dad, I always used to let Ben eat out of my hand. He expects it."

"You've done this before? Let him eat out of your hand?" his father asked.

Mark took heart and said, "Lots of times. Here, I'll show you." He reached for a slice of bread, then hesitated, looking at his father anxiously.

His father twisted around to face them, moving the rifle slightly, then said, "All right, show me. But take it easy."

Mark tore the bread into chunks and extended them to Ben in the palm of his hand. Ben lifted them one by one with a touch of lips and pink tongue that was as soft as velvet. Mark closed his hand over the last piece, and Ben nibbled delicately at his closed fist until Mark opened his hand with a sudden burst of laughter and gave it to him. He reached out and rubbed Ben's ears, and Ben twisted his head first right, then left so that Mark could scratch first one ear and then the other. "He likes being scratched under the chin most of all," Mark said. He stepped close and bent over the big furry head.

His father said sharply, "Mark!" But it was too late. Mark's hand was already scratching under Ben's broad chin, and Ben had stretched his neck as far and flat out as he could. His little eyes were closed blissfully, and he was grunting with pure delight.

"See, Dad?" Mark said happily. "See?"

"You've done this before, too?"

"Every day," Mark said. "Come on, Dad, you do it. See how he loves it."

"I can see fine from here." His father rose abruptly. "It's

time we were getting home. Your mother will be waiting supper for us."

They were silent as they went down the trail. Finally his father said, "I guess you didn't believe me when I told you that brownies are dangerous and unpredictable and that Ben is a wild animal no matter how tame he seems."

"Yes, sir, I do," Mark said. "But Ben doesn't act that way and I—I forget."

"You trust Ben. Is that it?"

"Yes. And he trusts me," Mark said.

"You two do seem to have some sort of understanding," his father agreed thoughtfully. "If I warned you again to be more careful, you'd probably just forget."

"I try, Dad. But with Ben, it's hard to remember."

"I can see that." His father said no more until they neared the house. Then, "I've got to know more about Ben, for your good as well as for my own peace of mind. I want to watch him, study his behavior. But not in the shed where he's been chained for almost five years. Maybe down at the creek where I found you two that first morning."

"You think Ben might act different down there?" Mark asked.

"It's possible. Perhaps a real tough brownie lurks beneath Ben's tame, gentle exterior. I want to see what he does when he gets the clean, sharp smell of the sea and the land in his nostrils, the feel of the earth beneath his feet, without that chain around his neck to hold him back."

"What do you think he'll do?" Mark asked.

"He might be like that circus bull elephant I read about. For ten years he traveled with the circus and seemed very tame and gentle. Then one night he broke out and almost wrecked a small town where they were playing. One taste of freedom, and they could never trust him again."

"Ben won't be like that," Mark said positively.

"That's what I want to find out. Tomorrow, when you get home from school, we'll take Ben down to the creek. He can get some exercise, a meal of grass and roots, and maybe we'll learn something."

When Mark came charging down the trail from school the next afternoon, his father was waiting on the porch, the ever-present rifle cradled in his arm. They went up to the shed together. His father stopped at the door and said, "You're sure you can lead Ben? That morning when you took him down to the creek to turn him loose, did you lead him, or was he pulling you along? Think now. This is important."

"I led him, Dad. Honest. I even made him run part of the way because I was afraid someone might see us."

"All right. Go in and untie him and take him down just as you did before. I'll be right behind you. And if he does anything, or if anything happens, get out of my way. Understand?"

"He won't do anything," Mark said confidently. "You'll see."

Mark went into the shed, unfastened the chain, and reappeared leading Ben. Ben blinked at the bright sunlight and swung his big head right and left as his nose sampled the clean spring air. "Come on." Mark pulled on the chain. "Come on, Ben." Ben dropped in at his heels like a dutiful dog and, with big shoulders rolling, head swinging, followed the boy off across the soft, spongy tundra. His father brought up the rear, rifle at the ready.

When they reached the creek bottom and the coarse, waist-high grass, his father said, "All right, Mark, this is a good place. Turn him loose. Let's see what happens."

"Nothing will happen," Mark said confidently. "He'll just eat like he did before when we were down here."

"That could have been one of those freak happenings," his father said. "Take the chain off. And don't get in front of me. Do just like you did before."

Mark unsnapped the chain and dropped it on the ground. Andersen stood back, tense, the rifle held across his chest in both hands. Now he would soon know what he could expect. All his fears and suspicions, all his years of knowledge of the great animals were focused on this moment.

Ben stood motionless, looking about. He padded off a few feet, sniffing explosively at grass clumps. Suddenly he stopped and reared to his full height, big forepaws hanging loosely before him, head swiveling as he looked about, actions typical of the brown bear when he is annoyed or uncertain or has found something that needs investigating. His whole body became tense and alert. He had discovered he was free.

Andersen knew what was happening to Ben. All the wild instincts that had been bred into the animal for centuries and had lain dormant during the years he'd been chained in the darkness of the shed were about to come violently alive.

Ben's sensitive ears and nose were hard at work. His delicate black nostrils, which could pick up the scent of another animal or an intruder two miles away, were greedily drawing in all the ancient smells of the earth. There were the mustiness of deep canyons, the cold bite of distant snow fields mingled with the pungent scent of the tundra, the soft breath of the sun-warmed earth that rose about him, all laced with the clean, salty tang of the sea. The sharp ears were picking up the distant thunder of the surf, the far-off cries of clouds of gulls, the near chatter of a jay, the raucous voice of a pair of crows, the scream of a fishing eagle, and the endless musical brawling of the nearby creek running over its stones. All these sounds and smells could mean but one thing to Ben, the thing that he had never known and that every wild animal has craved since time began: freedom—freedom to live as his kind had lived through the ages. Andersen shifted the rifle and eased back the bolt. Now! he thought. Now it's coming!

The next moment Ben dropped heavily back on all fours, sniffed into a grass clump, ripped it out, and stood chewing contentedly. Mark had both hands twisted in the long hair of his neck and was pulling. "That's tough," he was saying impatiently. "Come over here where it's tender."

Andersen watched his son and the huge animal move from grass clump to grass clump, going steadily up the creek, away from him. He lowered the rifle muzzle and let the bolt back carefully. His palms were wet; his chest ached. He realized he'd been holding his breath, and he let it out slowly. They were fifty feet off before he thought to follow.

Ben was not so starved now. Because he was particular of what he ate, he and Mark moved rapidly through the grass, hunting the most succulent tufts. Andersen tried to keep pace with them, but for seconds at a time they were all but lost to sight in the tall grass. A dozen times it was on his lips to call Mark back, to tell him not to get too close to Ben, to be careful. Then he would hear Mark's voice calling Ben off in another direction where he'd found a particularly tender clump, or he would be pulling roots from the edge of Ben's crunching jaws and laughing at him.

Andersen was still some fifty feet behind them when they entered the field of boulders. There was no high grass here, just a long sloping field dotted with huge rocks half buried in the

57

earth. They'd be easy to watch. He sat down, his back against a rock, the rifle across his knees.

Ben and Mark were already working on a huge half-buried boulder. Mark was pulling at a corner while Ben stood in front of him, head down, expectantly watching the rock. "Well, come on!" Mark panted. "I can't pull it up alone." After a little while, Ben stretched his big head and sniffed loudly around the edges of the rock. Apparently he caught a scent. His big paw scratched eagerly at the earth. His claws caught, and with an effortless heave the rock was torn from its bed in the earth and rolled aside. His paw slapped swiftly. There was a satisfied smacking of lips, and boy and bear moved toward another rock.

They were wrapped up in their activity, and seemed to have forgotten Andersen and the rifle. Mark was pouring a stream of talk at Ben, urging him to greater efforts, pushing his head aside when Ben became too anxious, or applauding when his catch was particularly good. Sometimes Ben sniffed at a rock and refused to become interested. Then they moved with one accord to another. Several times, as they worked together at a particularly large rock, the brown head of the boy and the golden taffy-brown head of the bear were side by side. Once, as a rock popped out of the earth, some small animal darted between Mark's legs, and escaped. Ben stood looking at the boy reprovingly, as if to say, "You let him get away." Mark's laugh was clear and happy. He scratched Ben's ears and beneath his broad chin. Then they went to another rock.

Andersen smiled, settled his shoulders more comfortably, and looked about. He heard the small sounds of wildlife about him, but the feeling of silence and solitude was very strong. The rock was warm; the earth gave back the heat of the day. He dug up a fistful of black earth and held it to his nose.

Ben's big paw scratched eagerly at the earth.

It smelled good; it smelled like things alive and growing. It smelled like spring. He let the earth trickle through his fingers.

A crow planed down a few feet off and walked to a hole Ben and Mark had left. It cocked its black head one way, then the other, the sharp eyes searching for something to eat. Then it walked to the next hole. A mother duck waddled from the grass, crossing between Andersen and the crow. She was followed by six downy yellow babies. They were all headed for the creek. They were so close he could see the babies' eyes. A gray fox appeared, stealthily following the ducks. He stopped suddenly, one forepaw held delicately aloft. His pointed ears shot forward; then, without a sound, he whirled and vanished back into the grass. A flock of gulls sailed overhead, wings fixed, letting the air currents ferry them back to the beach. He watched the gulls out of sight. It had been a long time since he'd just sat and done nothing, waiting to see what would happen or what would go by. Not since he'd been a kid—far too long. Man lost a lot in growing up.

Mark's laugh sounded out in the rock field, and Karl glanced up. Some small animal had probably eluded Ben again. They were getting rather far off. He'd get up soon and move out to them.

Mark's voice said, "Come on, Ben. You're full now. Your stomach feels like a basketball."

Andersen started and jerked his head up. Mark and Ben were coming toward him. Mark was in the lead, and Ben was padding at his heels with his pigeon-toed walk. Behind them, many more rocks had been turned up. Mark's hands and face were dirty and his knees caked with mud.

Andersen reached for the rifle, and discovered it had fallen from his knees to the ground. He retrieved it and rose, scrubbing a hand across his face and eyes. "Ben get a good feed?" he asked.

"Did he ever!" Mark patted Ben's bulging side. "Feel, Dad."

"I can see." Andersen dug out his watch. "We'd better be heading home. It's getting late. You remember where you left the chain? You and Ben lead off; I'll follow."

All that evening Andersen said nothing about the trip down to the creek in the afternoon. It was not until he and his wife had been in bed for some time and he had lain there staring at the black ceiling that he finally said, "Ellen?"

"Yes," she answered drowsily from the edge of sleep.

"About Ben and Mark—I watched 'em today. I mean I watched 'em part of the time."

"What?"

"I went to sleep on 'em," he confessed. "Only for a couple of minutes," he added hastily. "But I did drop off."

"Oh," Ellen said.

"I should have been wide awake every second. I meant to be." He was glad it was dark. He was embarrassed at what he was about to say. But it had been nagging at him all evening. "Out there this afternoon I sort of got the feeling that those two were in—well—some sort of world all their own. And I couldn't get in. You've got to have some special kind of boy—or bear—or something understanding to get in their world. I don't have it. I never will. It doesn't make sense, but they actually seemed to understand each other. It was the oddest feeling. It sort of lulled me into thinking everything was all right and I had nothing to worry about."

"That's good," Ellen said.

"It's not good at all," Karl exploded. "That's the whole trouble. When I watch them together I get a false sense of security. It's as if my common sense had gone to sleep. And that's dangerous. I know better. Ben's a wild animal, a brown bear! A brownie, Ellen! Do you understand what I'm trying to say?"

"Of course, dear." Ellen reached back and patted his hand reassuringly. "Now go to sleep," she murmured.

Karl lay there wide awake long after Ellen's even breathing told him she was asleep. It was strange that she did not seem the least worried about Mark and Ben's relationship. He finally raised himself on one elbow and looked down at her. She slept as peacefully as a child, one arm curved gracefully above her head, her smooth cheek pressed into the pillow.

It came to him with a shock why she could sleep so contentedly. She had the special understanding that made her a part of Mark and Ben's world—a world where there seemed to be no doubt or fear or worry. He could think of no better words to describe it than their "magic world." A world he would never understand or know about because he was a realist.

He lay down again, careful not to wake her. He hadn't formed a clean-cut decision concerning Ben. But since this afternoon he did feel better about him. On such slim comfort he finally fell asleep.

✕✕✕✕ 6 ✕✕✕✕

A T breakfast Mark's mother said, "Before the season opens and you men take off fishing, we've got to make hay for Ben's winter bed."

"How do you make hay?" Mark asked.

"That's easy for an old farmhand like your mother," his father said.

His mother smiled. "When you get home from school tonight, we'll go down to the creek where that long grass grows, and I'll show you."

"You'll need something to cut with," his father said. "I saw a scythe at the hardware store. I'll bring it home at noon."

"If we're going to the creek, can we take Ben?" Mark asked.

Ellen said, "I could take the rifle."

Karl shook his head. "You're a good shot, and I'm sure you'd be cool in an emergency; but I just can't see you facing an angry Ben, even with the most powerful rifle. I'd rather you had a man along. I can't go. They're having trouble with the retort at Western Fisheries, and I offered to help repair it. But Clearwater can go. Clearwater's a dead shot. And he probably knows as much about brownies as any man in the North."

Mark had known Clearwater all his life. He had been the crew years ago when Mark's grandfather was seining. Karl, at his father's death, had inherited the boat, and Clearwater as well. Karl often said Clearwater had taught him all he knew about seining. Clearwater's bunk aboard the *Far North* was his only home. His only interests were fishing and the Andersen family. The Andersen family, he insisted with his ever-ready good humor, was really his by right of discovery and promotion. It was Clearwater who had informed Mark's father that a new girl had come north to teach in Orca City's grade school, and he had told Karl that if he wanted to see a lady of quality and rare beauty, he should see the new teacher. Six months later, Karl Andersen married Ellen Richards. Clearwater was best man.

His real name was Henry something. But in the distant past someone had called him "Clearwater" for a reason now long forgotten, and the name had stuck. Now he was known by no other.

"I'll have Clearwater come up and go haying with you," Mark's father said.

"Fine," Ellen answered. She smiled at Mark. "Tonight, son, you'll learn how a farmer makes hay."

When Mark came hurrying down the trail and into the kitchen after school, Clearwater was sitting at the table, finishing a cup of coffee. He was short and broad, with a deep chest and powerful shoulders. "Clearwater should have been at least a six-footer," his father often said, "but his legs quit growing too soon." His face was round and full and deeply tanned. His bullet head held only a fringe of gray hair around the ears. Winter and summer he wore a black knit beret. In summer it protected his bald head from the sun and in winter kept it warm. He had merry gray eyes and a ready smile, but neither were in evidence today.

He finished his coffee, and rose. "All right. Let's get goin'," he said, and reached for the rifle.

The three of them went up the trail to the shed. Mark's

mother carried the new scythe. She was dressed in jeans and a man's light shirt, the sleeves rolled above her round, lightly tanned arms.

At the shed Clearwater said: "Your dad tells me you can handle this brute. All right, bring 'im out. But don't get in my way. Understand?"

"There won't be any trouble with Ben," Mark's mother said.

"Course not." Clearwater's voice was unusually harsh. "He's just a five-year-old brownie! As gentle as a day-old kitten."

When Mark brought Ben into the sunlight, Clearwater stepped back and studied Ben as the bear stood blinking in the bright sunlight, swinging his head and sampling the breeze. "All right," he said finally. "Take off, Mark."

Clearwater made Mark and Ben walk ahead. He came a few feet behind, rifle cradled in his arms, finger on the trigger. Mark's mother came last. The scythe was slung across her shoulder, and a small smile lifted her lips.

They crossed the soft, sun-warmed tundra with Ben lumbering along at his pigeon-toed gait, first behind, then beside Mark. Every few feet he stopped and thrust his inquisitive black nose into the tundra moss. Mark pulled at him, urging and scolding: "Come on. You know what that smells like. You don't eat tundra moss. We're going down to the creek where you can get grass and roots and things like that. Now, quit fooling around and come on." Ben seemed to understand, or else he decided there was nothing in the tundra moss to eat. He finally fell in beside Mark, and padded steadily along with no more stops to sniff and investigate.

They dropped over the rim of the tundra into the small valley where the creek ran and the long grass grew. Mark's mother said, "This is fine. This grass will make good hay."

Mark unsnapped the chain, and Clearwater said sharply, "You're not turnin' him loose?"

"He won't go far," Mark said.

"Well, why not?" Clearwater said grimly. "It'd take a dozen men to hold th' brute anyway."

Ben padded off a few feet, blew loudly into a tempting clump of grass, ripped it out, and began chewing with a great smacking of lips.

Clearwater stationed himself on guard on a small hump of ground, prepared to watch his three charges.

Mark and his mother paid no further attention to Ben or Clearwater. Ellen said: "This is the way you scythe grass, Mark. I did it often as a girl at home. The scythe is one of the oldest farm tools known. For thousands of years it was the only way man had to cut grasses and grains." She gripped the stubby handles and swung the scythe with a smooth, full-armed sweep. There was a sound like ripping cloth, and a narrow half-moon of grass fell smoothly before the flashing blade. She stepped forward, set her feet, and the scythe flashed again. There was the ripping sound, and the half-moon had doubled in size.

Mark watched for several minutes. Then she stopped and held out the scythe to him. "Don't try to use the full length of the blade. Cut with the last six inches or so. Try it."

Mark set himself, and swung. The point dug into the soft earth. He reached too far, took too wide a cut, and got less than half the grass. He swung too high, and the grass bent before the blade. It took some minutes to get the feel, for the timing and rhythm to come. Finally he laid down his first half-moon of grass. It was not as smooth as his mother's or as neat, but it was cut.

Scything, Mark discovered, was hard work. He soon tired. Then his mother took the scythe and cut grass while he rested. They took turns cutting for some time, and the field of mown grass grew rapidly.

They had stopped once to rest and survey their work when Clearwater left his mound and came over to them. "Feel kind of silly standin' there with a rifle, doin' nothin' while you two do all th' work," he explained.

"You're the guard," Mark's mother explained.

"Guard from what?" Clearwater asked. "Look over there."

A short way off, Ben had just finished a particularly succulent patch of grass and now gave every indication he was ready for his afternoon nap in the shade of a willow bush.

"You've decided he's tame and not dangerous?" Mark's mother asked.

"Nope," Clearwater said promptly. "Brownies 're untamable, unpredictable, and dangerous. But he's gonna take a nap for an hour at least, and he's right in plain sight where I can peek at him every few minutes. So I might as well make myself useful." He laid down the rifle and said, "Gimme that grass cutter. You two take it easy while I do some mowin'."

At first Clearwater did not do much better than Mark had done. But he concentrated on the job, and soon, because of his greater strength, the cut was smooth and even. He became fascinated watching the grass fall in a clean sweep before the blade. A drop of sweat formed at the band of his beret and tracked down his leather-brown cheek. He was smiling, enjoying himself, ripping the scythe through with mighty strokes, when there was an explosive "Whoof!" at his very heels. He had heard that sound many times before, and knew exactly what it meant. He dropped the scythe and dived for the rifle. His feet tangled in the long grass and he sprawled full length.

The beret bounced from his head and landed a few feet off. He rolled over frantically, gathered himself to spring erect—and froze.

Ben towered over him, his huge head bent down not more than a yard away. In all his years in the North, Clearwater had never looked into the face of a brownie this close, or looked up at one from a prone position. Ben looked immense, a veritable mountain of bone, muscle, and fur. Clearwater could see the black nostrils expand and contract as they sucked in the man scent. The big head stretched closer, and Ben's little eyes studied Clearwater.

Clearwater darted a glance at the rifle twenty feet away. He thought of springing to his feet and dashing for it, but he knew he'd never make it. Clearwater decided that his only chance was to lie perfectly still. In his sixty years in the North, he had come through many tight spots by refusing to panic.

He lay still and taut, staring back into Ben's eyes, his fingers digging into the soft earth while he waited. He waited for Ben's curiosity to be satisfied, for the bear to turn away, or for his nearness and the man scent to arouse the killing lust within him.

Then he heard Ellen's clear laugh and Mark's too, high and gleeful. The boy came running through the grass, threw an arm around Ben's neck, and stood laughing down at Clearwater. "He likes you. Ben likes you, Clearwater."

"He does?" Clearwater asked skeptically. "You can tell?"

"Of course." Mark was still laughing. "Just look at him."

Clearwater had every opportunity. The bear's lips were not drawn back to disclose long ugly teeth ready to rip and tear. He saw only the brownie's insatiable curiosity, and an apparent lack of fear of human scent.

"Pet him," Mark said, suiting the action by banging Ben

solidly between the eyes with his hand. "Go ahead, Clearwater; scratch his ears, like this. He likes it."

Clearwater was no coward. And here a slip of a boy with an arm about the brute's neck was urging him on confidently. And behind them stood Ellen, hands on hips, smiling. Clearwater carefully stretched forth a hand and touched Ben's ear. Nothing happened. He scratched tentatively. Ben rolled his big head, so that Clearwater automatically scratched first one ear, then the other.

"He likes being scratched under the chin most," Mark volunteered. "Scratch him under the chin, Clearwater."

More confident, Clearwater thrust his hand under the massive chin and raked his stubby fingers through the coarse hair.

"Harder, scratch harder," Mark urged.

Ben flattened his head, stretched his neck, and moved closer until his black nose was no more than a foot from Clearwater's chest. He closed his eyes blissfully and began grunting like a pig, with pure delight. Clearwater looked at Mark and at Ellen. He began to grin. He scratched harder. Then he suddenly laughed outright. His other hand came forward and patted Ben between the eyes as he'd seen Mark do. "Benjamin"—he laughed delightedly—"you're quite a boy. Yes, siree, so help me Hannah! You're quite a boy!" He gave Ben a final pat, a final scratch, and scrambled up.

Ben thrust his nose up at Clearwater, sucked in a single explosive sniff, then turned and padded off. Clearwater retrieved his beret and the scythe, and stood watching Ben, who had stopped to dig up a skunk-cabbage root.

Ellen asked quietly, "A tame brownie, Clearwater?"

"What else?" Clearwater agreed. He punched the beret back on his head. "Forty years I been around these brutes, and now I find I don't know a thing about 'em. How about that?"

They worked another hour, the three of them taking turns scything. Ben wandered among them, hunting tender shoots and digging roots.

Finally Mark's mother stopped and wearily surveyed the field of cut grass. "We've got enough," she said. "Tomorrow we can gather it into piles. You'll have to haul it before you go fishing. If it rains, it'll spoil."

"I'll borrow a four-wheel pickup and we'll haul day after tomorrow," Clearwater said. "Season opens in four days. We've got to leave the day before to get on th' fishin' grounds."

"I can help," Mark said. "We have to go back to school only for report cards."

When they were ready to leave, Clearwater could not find the rifle. They hunted about, kicking through the mown grass. Ben finally found it. Some faint aroma of burned powder or gun oil touched his delicate nostrils, and curiosity sent him digging through layers of fresh-cut grass. Clearwater saw him pawing and sniffing at the muzzle of the rifle. "Fine guard," he grumbled to Mark's mother. "Can't even keep track of th' rifle." He patted Ben, and said, "Nice goin', pal."

Mark put the chain on Ben, and they trudged off across the tundra toward home. This time Clearwater carried both the rifle and the scythe.

The next day, when they went to the shed to get Ben, Clearwater was his old cheerful, humorous self. "Go on," he airily waved Mark on, "get our big friend out here. We got to put th' show on th' road."

Their trip to the creek had the carefree air of a pleasure jaunt. They walked four abreast, with Mark and Ben in the

70

middle. Ben padded along beside Clearwater, not stopping or holding back to sniff and paw at the tundra moss, but hurrying straight for the spot where the land dipped down to the valley floor.

"Will you get a look at th' big lug pickin' 'em up and layin' 'em down?" Clearwater laughed. He patted the hump between Ben's shoulders, "You know where you're goin', don'tcha, Benjamin?"

The moment Mark removed Ben's chain at the valley floor, the ancient wisdom born into his breed centuries ago came alive in Ben. He rose to his imposing height on his hind legs and stood swinging his head, sensitive nostrils casting for wayward scents, sharp ears attuned to the sounds of the earth. Suddenly he dropped back on all fours and went crashing straight through the brush for the creek.

Clearwater looked at the retreating Ben, and said in a sharp voice, "Hey! Come on. Come on!"

When they burst through the grass and brush to the creek, Ben was looking down into the clear rushing water. He tapped at the water with a big paw, and his black nose quested along its surface with excited snortings.

Mark and Clearwater ran to the bank and peered down. A foot beneath the surface Mark saw a thin line of slim torpedo shapes fighting their way upstream.

This, Mark knew, was what the North had waited a year for. This had been the cause of the boiling activity up and down the coast the past weeks. It had brought the eleven hundred seiners crowding into Orca City's bay and had packed the town with strangers until it could not hold them all.

Clearwater snatched off his beret, hurled it into the air, and let go with a full-lunged cry that was to raise excitement to fever pitch aboard boats, in canneries, in homes, and along the streets of every small town for a thousand miles up and down the Alaskan coast.

"Salmon!" Clearwater shouted. "Th' salmon 're here!" He pointed into the water excitedly. "Look at 'em! There they are. Th' vanguard of th' run. That means th' run is waitin', millions of 'em millin' around a few miles off th' coast, gettin' ready to come in. It can hit any day, any hour. So help me Hannah! Ain't that a sight?" Even an old-timer like Clearwater was awed at this miracle that happened almost to the day and hour each year, when the great horde of salmon boiled in from the mysterious reaches of the sea.

Clearwater patted Ben's solid shoulder. "You knew, Benjamin. Even before we *got* here, you knew." He scratched his bald head thoughtfully. "How much more do you know that I don't know? I'm wonderin', Benjamin. I'm really wonderin'."

"He wants a salmon," Mark said. "You can see he wants one."

"And he don't know how to catch it," Clearwater said. "Brownie cubs learn from their mamas, and Fog Benson killed Ben's mama."

"Then we have to teach him. How do we teach him, Clearwater?"

"You got me."

"How does a brownie catch fish?" Ellen asked.

"Mostly they wade out and stand there till a salmon swims close. Then they plunge their heads in and grab him."

"If we can catch a salmon we can teach him."

"That's easy." Clearwater laid the rifle on the bank, unbuckled his trousers belt and made a loop of it, using the buckle for a slip knot. He stretched flat on the bank, lowered the loop into the water, and waited for a salmon to stray close. Soon a solitary salmon quested along the pebbly bottom to-

72

ward them. Clearwater moved the loop directly in the salm-on's path. Leisurely, the salmon started through. With a jerk, Clearwater landed the salmon flopping on the bank. He scooped it up, dashed it against a rock, and killed it. He handed it to Mark's mother.

She gave it to Mark. "Wade out a few feet," she said. "Let Ben see it and call him. When he comes to get it, sink the salmon about a foot underwater, or as deep as that line is swimming. We want him to plunge his head down after it. Don't let him have it on the surface. Make him duck his head. Then he'll think he's caught his own fish. And, Mark, hold the salmon by the tail. Ben's excited, and might grab your hand by mistake."

Mark waded into the creek, held up the salmon so that Ben could see it, and called, "Come on, Ben." He swung the salmon. "Come and get it, Ben. Come on."

Ben looked at the salmon flashing silvery in the sunlight. He put a paw into the water, then drew it out. He sniffed loudly, reaching for the salmon's scent.

"Come on," Mark urged. "Come on, Ben."

Ben put a paw into the water again. The other followed. He took another step deeper into the creek. Suddenly he plunged in, splashing eagerly toward Mark, his little eyes fastened greedily on the swinging salmon.

While Ben was still a step away, Mark thrust his arm into the water. Ben looked at the salmon a foot beneath the surface. He pushed his nose into the water, lifted it, and blew mightily. Mark raised the salmon nearer the surface. The swift current undulated the salmon's body, making it look alive and temptingly close. "Hurry up." Mark shoved down on Ben's head with his free hand. Without warning, Ben plunged his head into the water and his teeth clamped down on the salmon's back. He splashed ashore, dropped the salmon on the bank, put a paw on its tail and ripped it in two with a twist of big jaws. Fresh salmon is a brownie's favorite food, and this was the first Ben had ever tasted. He dispatched it in a half dozen bites, and looked expectantly at Mark for more.

"You'll have to wade out with him. He doesn't realize he can catch them alone," his mother said.

Mark waded into the creek, and Ben splashed eagerly after him.

They stood still, the water boiling about their legs. The migrating salmon, intent only on spawning, saw nothing to frighten them, and cruised close by. Ben became excited. His black nose twitched in anticipation. He flailed a big paw at the fish, momentarily frightening them. He thrust his nose into the water and jerked it out again. "Go on," Mark coaxed. "Stick your head down and grab one. All brownies do it." He wiggled his hand in the water under Ben's nose. He shoved down on Ben's head. "Go on, Ben. Go on."

Whether Ben understood, or whether the sight of the salmon so near was too much, he suddenly plunged his head into the water and came up with a salmon wriggling in his jaws. He marched triumphantly ashore with his prize to the accompaniment of Mark's and his mother's clapping, and Clearwater's praise, "Nice goin', Benjamin. That was done like a true brownie."

They watched Ben catch and eat another fish before they left him and returned to the hayfield.

It took almost two hours to gather and pile the grass they'd scythed. When they finished, Ben was nowhere in sight. They found him still on the creekbank. He'd gorged himself on salmon, but, unable to leave such a wonderful feast, he'd gone to sleep right there, with one big forepaw trailing in the water.

74

Hauling the hay with the pickup was no problem. By evening of the next day, Mark and Clearwater had it all neatly piled in a corner of Ben's shed.

The following morning Mark visited the three restaurants with the wheelbarrow to gather up their scraps for the last time.

His father and Clearwater made final preparations on board the *Far North*. They stored cases of food and bedding and filled the water and fuel tanks. Mark's mother got out his raincoat and sou'wester hat. That night he took them down to the *Far North*.

Clearwater was lying in his bunk, reading. The light glistened on his bald head and reflected in the rolls of muscles across his broad back and shoulders. "I guess you're kind of excited about your first time out, huh?" he asked.

"Yes, sir," Mark said.

"Me too. I been goin' for forty years. But when we head out th' first mornin' it gives me th' same lift I got th' very first time. You'll like it, Mark."

Lying in bed that night, Mark wasn't so sure. He had never been away from home for even a single night. He had never slept in any other bed. It had been easy to promise his father he would go. He had thought it would be a great adventure, like it had been for Jamie. Now it didn't seem so great. Maybe he couldn't take a man's place aboard the boat. But of course he'd try. This was part of the bargain that had saved Ben's life. That was the most important thing. Saving Ben had been the best thing he'd ever done.

Next morning the last thing he did was run up and tell Ben good-bye. "I'll be back soon," he promised, scratching Ben under the chin. "I don't want to go, but I have to so I can keep you. You be good, and I'll bring you a whole sack of salmon."

Ben licked Mark's fingers, looking for something to eat; finding nothing, he pushed at the boy's hands with his nose, then raised his head and sniffed at his face. Mark patted his head.

"I'll be back soon. I'll be back."

Ben followed to the end of the chain and stood looking out the door as Mark ran down the trail to the house.

His mother went to the dock with them. Half the seiners in the bay were gone already. By night there would be none left. They would be scattered over thousands of miles of sea, awaiting the official opening of the season, 6:00 A.M. tomorrow morning.

Karl Andersen kissed his wife, and said, "Be back soon. You be careful with Ben. Hear?"

Ellen smiled, ruffling his cotton-blond hair. "You be careful, too. Good husbands are hard to find."

"Maybe I should be a bookkeeper or something," Karl said.

"You, in an office at a desk? You wouldn't be Karl Andersen."

She kissed Mark and held him close. "It's going to be fine with your father and Clearwater." She smoothed his hair with her fingers, her brown eyes suddenly bright. "You've grown up a lot the past weeks. Don't rush it, darling. Don't rush it too much."

"I won't, Mother," Mark said uncertainly. "You be sure and feed Ben enough." The engine of the *Far North* started with an explosive kick and a burst of blue exhaust fumes. He turned, ran down the gangplank, and jumped aboard.

His mother called to Clearwater, "You take care of my men."

Clearwater lifted his beret, his smile big and white. "Don't I always?"

The *Far North* slipped away from the dock and headed out into the bay.

Mark leaned against the seine pile in the stern and waved to his mother. She stood on the edge of the dock, small and slender and very straight, and waved back. He watched her grow smaller. There was a terrible emptiness inside him. He lifted his eyes above the roofs of the town. He could see their home, a white splash against the green and yellow tundra. He could not see Ben's shed at all.

A HUNDRED miles from Orca City they anchored for the night in a quiet cove. It was the first night Mark had ever spent aboard the boat, and he could not sleep for the strangeness of it all. Even though the ports were open and the cool night air poured in, it could not dispel the heavy smell of hot metal and burned oil and fuel that came from the nearby engine.

Through the open port he could see the pale northern sky and a single star. By raising himself he could see the sea, black and mysterious, and the frowning height of the mountains rising sheer behind the nearby beach.

In his bunk across the narrow aisle, Clearwater lay flat on his back, thick arms folded across his broad chest, the beret tipped forward almost to his eyes. He had been snoring steadily for an hour. Beyond, Mark could make out the shape of his father's head. He wondered if his father was asleep, too.

At home he'd been accustomed to complete silence at night. Here the night was alive with strange sounds. There was the muffled lap of water against the hull, the creaking of the fender against the dolphin as the boat gently rose and fell on the bosom of the sea. A whale blew nearby, then another and another, the sound like air hissing from a tire. Whales seemed to be all about the Far North. To visualize them rolling out of the depths was frightening. Clearwater had said that there was something growing on the bottom here that whales loved, and they came in here to feed. In times past Clearwater had often felt them bump against the bottom of the boat.

Mark waited fearfully for the solid thump of a whale surfacing beneath the keel or against the side of the boat. A night bird cried suddenly across the cove, plaintive and mournful. A fox barked in quick little stabs of sound. Then there was silence—silence that exploded into full-throated sound on the nearby beach, filling the night with snarls, growls, and bawls. It jerked Mark upright in his bunk as fear gushed through him. It was the voice of the wild, of the primitive, of the mysterious sea and the forbidding mountains.

His father's voice said, "Hear that, Mark?"

"Yes," Mark managed.

"Couple of bears, probably fighting over a salmon. They make quite a racket, don't they?"

"Yes," Mark said. He visualized the fury of the fight. Never had he heard such savagery of sound. After a while the fight died away in squalls and growls.

Clearwater slept through it all, snoring peacefully.

There was the sound of his father rising. Then his tall shape loomed beside Mark's bunk. He lowered himself to the edge of the bunk and said: "I guess it seems kind of strange, even a little scary the first night or so. It was for Jamie. Was for me, too. I remember the first time I went out with my father and Clearwater. I didn't sleep a wink."

Mark had never heard his father's voice so gentle and understanding.

"You too, Dad?" he asked, surprised.

"It gets everybody the first time. Clearwater'd tell you the same if he was awake. But there's nothing to worry about."

"Not even the whales? Clearwater said he'd felt them bump the bottom of the boat."

"Sure. And it scares them more than it does us. They don't like to feel anything solid. They get away fast. They're really very timid. And no whale on earth would want to tip over the *Far North*. She's too big. You're as safe here as you would be at home in bed. A week from now you'll look forward to hearing all those night sounds."

"I will?"

"Of course. Every sound will be an old friend telling you everything's going along just as it should out there."

Mark slid down in bed again. He felt a sudden rush of warmth and closeness for his father he had never known before. He reached out and touched his father's arm. "Thanks, Dad," he said.

His father's big hand pressed his shoulder. "Everything all right?"

"Everything's fine," Mark said.

"Good boy." His father rose and went back to his own bunk.

Mark listened to the steady lapping against the hull. The night bird again trailed its eerie voice across the cove. The last sound he heard was the squeaking of the fender rubbing against the dolphin.

The throb of the motor wakened Mark. Bright sunlight poured through the ports, and there was the sound of curling water at the bow. The *Far North* was boring through the sea. He dressed hurriedly, remembering to slip into the orange life jacket his father had given him yesterday.

"When you show me you can swim, we'll get rid of this. Until then, you wear it every minute you're aboard the boat."

He entered the warm galley. The connecting door into the wheelhouse was open, and his father glanced back and called, "Your breakfast's on the stove, Mark. Hurry up and eat. Then you can climb on top and spot for a school. Season opens in an hour."

He found the same breakfast he'd had at home: cereal, an egg, toast, and a big glass of milk. When he'd finished, he carefully stacked the dishes in the sink and climbed to the top of the wheelhouse. Clearwater was there, scanning the flat, shining sea. He had tipped the black beret forward almost to his eyes, as if that would help shade them.

Several miles ahead, another boat was traveling in the same direction.

Mark asked, "How do you spot a school, Clearwater?"

"Look for jumpers. When you see salmon jumpin', there's a school."

"Are they all big schools?"

"Might be only a few hundred. Might be ten thousand or more. But if they're jumpin' over a big area, th' chances are you're into a big one."

Mark stood beside Clearwater, and watched, squinting his eyes against the silvery shine of the water. A big fish came out of the depths and began cutting slashing strokes across the bow. It was so shallow its dorsal fin sliced the surface with a sound like that of tearing silk. Mark said excitedly, "Clearwater, look!"

"Porpoise!" Clearwater clapped Mark on the shoulder. "That's good luck. We'll get a school sure now."

A few minutes later his father's blond head came out the pilothouse window below. "Six o'clock," he called. "Season's open. I think that boat ahead's got a set."

"What's a 'set'?" Mark asked Clearwater.

"He's spotted a school and is gonna run out his seine and gather 'em in."

They were closing on the boat ahead, and Mark could

observe what was going on. He saw an occasional silvery flash as a salmon shot out of the water and plunged back into the sea. A skiff took off from the seiner, the man rowing a circle around the school, dragging the seine after him.

"Too slow," Clearwater scoffed. "We use a motor."

They left the seiner astern. Several times they saw other boats in the distance, but none seemed to have a set.

An hour later they spotted their first jumpers, and Mark and Clearwater both shouted.

Clearwater climbed down to the deck and went aft to the skiff.

Five minutes later they were into the school, and salmon were flashing all about the *Far North*. "A big one!" Clearwater said gleefully. "A load!" He jumped into the skiff, started the outboard motor, and, carrying the end of the seine, roared off in a great circle, dragging the nine-hundred-foot seine off the stern into the sea after him. He completed the circle back at the stern of the *Far North*. Then they began hauling it in, closing the circle, pinching the trapped salmon into a tighter and tighter enclosure.

During this operation it was Mark's job to see that the seine was piled neatly on the turntable, ready to run out for the next set without tangling. When the enclosure was no more than fifty feet or so across, Mark could see the salmon, a solid mass, churning and flashing in their confinement.

The brail, a giant dip net that could lift four hundred salmon at a time and that was operated from a boom aboard the boat, was run out. Clearwater guided it into the mass of fish. When it was full, the winch lifted the net, cascading water and stretched taut with its load of gasping fish. Mark steered the brail over the open hatch. His father lowered it into the hold and emptied it.

An hour later they had finished. Both hatches were filled to the top with squirming salmon. Mark was soaked, and his arms and shoulders ached from pushing the loaded brail over the hold and steering it down inside.

Clearwater said, "Ten thousand at least." He grinned at Mark. "Didn't I tell you that dolphin would bring us luck? They always do."

Mark's father put a hand on his shoulder and smiled down at him. "You did fine. Now get below and take off those wet clothes. There's nothing to do until we get to the cannery."

"We're going home to Orca City now?" Mark asked hopefully.

His father answered, speaking to Clearwater: "It's a day's run to Orca City. No use wasting all that time traveling this early in the day. We're two hours from the Butteville Cannery. We'll leave this load there. We might still pick up another one today."

Butteville was an old town with a gold-rush history. But the gold and prospectors had long since departed. Now it consisted of the cannery, a scattering of old houses where a few trappers, fishermen, and die-hard prospectors lived, and one store.

They tied to the dock below the conveyor, and his father said, "Mark, when they start the conveyor you help Clearwater until I get back. I've got to go up to the cannery office."

A minute later the conveyor belt began to run. Clearwater showed Mark how to use the pugh, a pole with a sharp steel tip with which you speared the fish out of the hold and tossed them onto the belt. The fish counter, a man with an automatic counting device, stood above them and tallied each salmon as it was tossed up.

Mark's father dropped down the ladder a little later and took the pugh from Mark. "There's a store here," he said. "Why don't you go up and make a deal to buy their old bread for Ben? Try to make a good one. Remember, it's bread they can't sell."

"How do you make a good deal?" Mark asked.

His father sat down on the edge of the hatch. Clearwater stopped pughing salmon and squatted on the second hatch.

"He'll ask more for that old bread than he expects to get. You offer less than you intend to pay. You both know he can't sell it. Then he comes down a little and you go up a little. That way you eventually arrive at a mutual price. Understand?"

"I'm not sure," Mark said doubtfully.

"It's like this," Clearwater cut in. He thumbed the beret onto the back of his head. "He hopes you'll pay a dime a loaf. So he asks maybe twelve cents. You figure it's worth nine or ten. You offer six. You argue—you for six, him for twelve. Finally you say seven. He comes down and says make it eleven. You don't go for eleven. He makes it ten and says your seven is 'way too low. You come up to eight—"

"Hey!" the fish counter yelled above them. "You gonna unload those fish or not?"

"In a minute," Clearwater said with dignity. "We got a problem in high finance. Now, where was I? Oh, yeah, there's two cents between you. Finally one of you says we'll split it. Make it nine and it's a deal. You got it for what you figured. He got a penny less."

"And remember," his father said, "he was going to throw that bread away. You didn't cheat him. You struck a good bargain."

"In a manner of speakin', you could say he even made a profit," Clearwater said.

"Another thing," his father cautioned. "Don't appear anxious."

"Act like you don't care a darn if you get it or not," Clearwater said.

The two men watched the boy climb to the dock; then they grinned at each other and went back to tossing fish.

The store was an old ramshackle building from the mining days. Workclothes, picks, axes, and other hardware were stacked about on open shelves with an assortment of foods.

When Mark told Mr. Ames what he wanted, the little storekeeper leaned over the counter, adjusted a pair of old-fashioned steel-rimmed glasses and inspected Mark with mild blue eyes. "Well, young man," he said, "possibly we can do some business. We do have a little old bread. But it's mostly pastries we have left over. Don't really pay to carry it, but some customers call for the stuff. There's nothing wrong with pastry for a bear. They like sweets, y' know."

"Yes, sir," Mark said. "I know."

"For th' bread"—Mr. Ames cleared his throat and glanced at his plump gray-haired wife farther down the counter—"it costs us twenty cents delivered. Th' pastry is different prices. Th' rolls 're fifty cents a dozen, th' cookies twenty-five, thirty, and thirty-five."

Mark tried to remember all the things his father and Clearwater had told him. "I could give you five cents a loaf for the old bread," he ventured.

"I was thinkin' ten would be about right," Mr. Ames said.

"You'll just have to throw it away," Mark said. "I could maybe give you six."

"Not for a while yet," Mr. Ames said. "Bread keeps a long time in these wrappers. Tell you what, for you I'll make it nine."

Here Mrs. Ames leaned her plump arms on the counter and smiled at Mark. "Let me settle this," she suggested. "I'm the disinterested third party. That's kind of legal talk," she explained to Mark. "Means I'm not included in this deal, so I can make a settlement fair to both of you. You're pretty sharp. You know you'll have to pay more than five. Amos here knows he'll have to take less than ten. Now then, you're only three cents apart. We can split it and make it seven and a half. But I don't like fooling with half cents. Make it seven all around."

Mr. Ames adjusted his glasses automatically. "He's getting the best of th' deal. But, all right."

Mrs. Ames smiled at Mark. "That's an awful good deal."

"Yes, ma'am," Mark said. "That's fine."

"Now about the pastry and old cookies."

"The bread is mostly what I wanted. Cookies would be awful expensive for Ben. He eats a lot," Mark explained.

"He does, if he's as big as your dad sa—"

"—Ten cents a dozen, rolls, cookies, all the pastry," Mrs. Ames said quickly. "Okay?"

Mark was tempted to say eight and settle for nine. But he decided not to. Ten cents was awfully cheap for rolls and cookies. "Yes, ma'am," he said. "When can I pick it up?"

"Next time you come by we'll have it in a sack for you," Mr. Ames said.

Back aboard the boat, Mark explained the deal he had made to his father. His father nodded gravely, "It was a good bargain for both of you. Now you need a freeze room to keep it in so it won't mold. Northern Fisheries has the only one in Orca City. I'll talk with Mike Kelly when we get in. Maybe we can make a deal to keep it there."

It was late in the evening when they spotted the next school.

This time Mark knew exactly what to do, and the job went off smoothly. When they had finished, the sun had set behind the Aleutian Range and pale northern twilight lay over the sea. His father decided to run all night and arrive at the Northern Fisheries dock in Orca City in the morning.

Mark went to sleep with the motor throbbing a few feet away. It was a sound he loved now. With every turn of the engine he was that much nearer home.

The moment they tied up the next morning, Mark climbed the stairs to the dock, carrying a gunny sack with a half dozen salmon for Ben. He had been gone two days and a night, but it seemed much longer. He felt he had changed a lot. He felt as old, as experienced, as wise as Jamie had seemed that last year when he'd gone on the boat with their father. He knew he was not the same boy who had kissed his mother good-bye on the dock and then run aboard the boat so she wouldn't see the tears filling his eyes.

His mother was sweeping the kitchen floor when he entered. She dropped the broom and hugged him hard. Then she held him off at arm's length, smiling, her eyes shining. "My," she said proudly. "My." Mark guessed she saw a difference in him, too.

He asked, "How's Ben, Mother? Did you have any trouble feeding him?"

She shook her dark, smooth head. "No trouble. Ben's a gentleman. My, you look good!"

"I've got to run up and see him, Mother. I brought him some salmon. I've got to be back at the boat in an hour."

"Then hurry up." She laughed and pushed him out the door. "When you come back I'll walk down to the dock with you. And Mark," she called after him, "don't interfere with Ben while he's eating the salmon. Understand?"

"Yes, Mother," he answered, and ran up the trail, the sack bumping his heels.

Ben had heard him coming and was straining at the length of the chain. Mark dropped the sack at the door, went in, and put his arms around Ben's big neck. He scratched his ears and under his chin. "I missed you," he said. "Did you miss me or just miss going to the creek for fish and grass?"

Ben sniffed at him and pushed his black nose against his hands, looking for food. His nose trapped the faint scent of the salmon at the door, and he stretched the chain taut, reaching toward it.

Mark emptied the sack before him and said, "There's six nice ones for you."

Ben went after the salmon with noisy pleasure. He paid no further attention to Mark. Mark watched him eat all but the heads and gill plates of two of the salmon. Then he gave Ben a pat and said, "I've got to go. I'll see you in a day or two and bring you some more."

When Mark and his mother reached the dock, Clearwater and his father had finished unloading the *Far North* and his father was climbing the steps to the dock. He kissed Ellen and said, "Two loads already, one really big. Mark's brought us luck."

"That's wonderful," his mother said. "How soon will you leave?"

"Right after I talk with Kelly. We need a cold place to keep Ben's bread so it won't mold. Northern Fisheries has the only freeze room around."

"Oh, my!" Mark's mother said. "That Mr. Kelly."

"I know." There was a grim note in his father's voice.

Mark had heard his father and Clearwater talk about Mike Kelly. He was the superintendent of Northern Fisheries, and the biggest man in Orca City. Mark had seen him from a distance, a huge, barrel-chested man, with a heavy thatch of coal-black hair and scowling black brows. His broad face had a faint blue cast that the closest shave could not erase. His black eyes were direct, and so cold and unfriendly that Clearwater said they made most men uncomfortable. In the three years Kelly had been here, he had made no friends and had no close associates. He went his lone way, doing his job, asking no favors or kindnesses, and giving none.

Mark sat at the galley table with Clearwater, watching his mother make sandwiches for them and wondering how his father was getting along with Kelly.

When his father returned a few minutes later, one look at his flushed face and stormy blue eyes and Mark didn't have to ask.

Mark's mother said, "It didn't go so well, did it?"

"That Kelly!" His father gritted his teeth and shook his head. "That bullhead."

"What happened?" Clearwater asked.

"I went to his office," Mark's father said. "I laid it out to him as friendly as I knew how, why we needed the cold room, about how much space we'd use. I offered to pay whatever he asked for the space and electricity we'd use. He just sat there behind that big desk like a block of granite and scowled at me. When I got all through, you know what he said?" Mark's father made his voice deep, like Kelly's, and mimicked, " 'I've got no time for stuff like that. This's a cannery. Not a kid's nursery school. I'm interested in putting up fifty thousand cases of salmon, and that's all.'

"Well, I started to leave. I had to leave or I'd have hit him. Then he said, 'Andersen, what're you using for brains? letting your kid run around with a brown bear.'

"That was more than I could take. I started to tell him off." His father dug his fingers angrily through his hair and shook his head. "The next thing I knew I was telling Kelly what Dr. Walker feared for Mark and how, as a last resort, we'd bought Ben. I don't know why I told him that, unless I felt that somehow I had to justify our crazy actions in getting Ben. I wound up telling him I didn't expect him to understand and that the only thing he could understand was fifty thousand cases of fish. Then I walked out. That man always could rile me," Mark's father admitted ruefully. "I just don't know why."

"What will we do, Dad?" Mark asked.

"I don't know yet," his father said. "We'll have to try and figure some other way. We've got to have some way of keeping that food cold."

They were still in the galley some minutes later when a voice shouted down from the dock above, "You! aboard the *Far North*. Where's Mark Andersen?"

Mark's father stepped outside and said, "In here, Kelly."

"Come up here, Mark Andersen," Kelly ordered.

Mark climbed the steps to the dock and stood looking up at the scowling Mike Kelly. He saw a big man, as tall as his father, but broader, thicker. He looked tough and mean with his black-browed scowl, his big fists jammed on his hips. But Mark saw no meanness in the big man's black eyes. Surprisingly, he was not afraid of Mike Kelly.

Kelly said, "I hear you've got a problem. Want to tell me about it?"

"It's Ben," Mark explained. "My bear. I have to get food for him this winter, dry bread and such. I get it at stores and bakeries where we stop. But I have to keep it in a cold place so it won't mold."

"And you'd like to use my freeze room?"

"Dad says your freeze room is big enough, and I'd pack it real tight so it wouldn't take up too much space."

"That's a big bear you've got. He'll eat a lot. It's going to take a lot of room no matter how tight you pack it," Kelly pointed out.

"He'll sleep most of the winter," Mark argued. "He'll only eat when he wakes up, so it won't take so much."

"You've got a point there," Kelly agreed soberly. He rubbed his jaw with a big hand, "Tell you what. For four dollars a month to help pay for the electricity to run the freezer, you've got a deal."

"Four dollars?" Mark's heart sank. "Every month?"

"The freezer has to run steadily," Kelly pointed out, "otherwise your bread'll thaw and mold."

Mark bit his lip. It might as well be four thousand. He was no better off than when Kelly had flatly said, "No."

"Of course," Kelly said, "that don't have to be cash. You can work it out—say—one Saturday a month. You can sweep out the office and dust out the place. Keep it clean during the shutdown. They're always yelling down in Seattle to keep the place looking nice. What do you say? We got a deal?" Kelly held out a huge hand.

Mark grasped it and they shook gravely. "Gee!" Mark beamed. "Thanks. Thanks a lot, Mr. Kelly."

"My father's name was Mr. Kelly," the big man said. "Mine is Mike. You remember that."

"Yes, sir, Mr. Kelly. I mean Mike."

"Good enough. You can start putting bread in the freezer any time you like." Kelly turned and strode away.

Mark's father ran up the stairs and stopped Kelly. "I appreciate what you've done, Kelly," he said. "But four dollars won't begin to pay the electric bill. And who ever heard of sweeping a cannery office in the middle of the winter?"

"You just heard it," Kelly said coldly. "And I say four dollars will pay for the juice he uses."

"Let me know what it really is," Mark's father said. "I'll pay the bill."

"You're sticking your nose where it don't belong," Kelly said bluntly. "And I hate nosy people. You tried to make a deal with me, and couldn't. Your kid did make a deal. He's satisfied and so am I. Now you back off. My deal's with Mark Andersen, not Karl Andersen. Why don't you tend to your seining and let me run this cannery?"

Karl Andersen smiled into Kelly's black eyes. "So your father's name was Mr. Kelly," he said. "All right, Mike, I apologize for offering payment. I should have known better. And I think I'll take your advice and stick to seining. You and Mark have things pretty well under control."

✕✕✕ 8 ✕✕✕

As often happens in the salmon industry, the run stopped completely the next day. For some mysterious reason unknown to man, the hordes of salmon remained somewhere at sea, far beyond the seiners' nets. The brown bears tramped the stream banks in vain. Finally hunger drove the titans back to the long, succulent grass of the meadows, to digging roots in the marshy spots and ripping open rotting stumps, or rolling rocks along the hillsides in search of small rodents, grubs, and ants. Foxes slunk along the streams searching for a forgotten dead salmon or for one that had come too near shore and was marooned in a shallow pool. The clouds of gulls that had hovered over the brown bears, waiting for their leavings, finally returned to the beach. Even the fishing eagle's uncannily sharp eyes could find no salmon as he endlessly cruised low over the spawning streams, screaming out his frustration and anger.

All across the Sound the fish traps were empty. The cannery doors remained hopefully open, but the crews lounged about, fishing off the docks, hiking across the tundra, playing cards, doing anything to pass the time while they waited for the run to hit again. Only a few of the eleven hundred seiners in the Sound caught enough to make gas money. The *Far North* was one of these.

Clearwater was not discouraged. "This's nothin' new. We've been through it before, plenty of times. They always hit again. Wait and see."

"We haven't seen a porpoise in a long time," Mark said.

"There you are!" Clearwater said. "There's your answer. We need to see a porpoise."

They saw the porpoise, but it did no good. Mark pointed this out, and Clearwater answered readily, "Temporarily postponed. But the run'll come. We just got to keep goin' till it hits again."

And so they did.

The *Far North* ranged far and wide. But as Mark's father said, "We couldn't buy a load for love nor money." They caught just enough barely to pay the gas bill and to feed Ben a few fish on weekends. They kept looking, making sets now when they saw only one or two jumpers. Each time Mark looked anxiously into the pocket when they'd pulled the seine close, hoping to see thousands of salmon milling inside.

They spent the nights anchored in small, quiet bays that Mark's father chose carefully so that Mark could go ashore and practice swimming. Mark worked hard at learning to swim. He had a greater reason than just the promise to his father that he'd learn this summer. He wanted to be free of the orange life jacket his father insisted he wear at all times aboard the boat. It was a badge telling everyone on the Sound he couldn't swim.

"It's like a billboard," Clearwater pointed out. "It says to everybody, 'Look, here's only half a sailor.' We got to get rid of this billboard."

During these daily lessons his father would sit on the beach or in the bow of the *Far North* and shout advice. Clearwater, stripped to the waist, waded into the water with Mark. With the ever-present beret clamped firmly on his round, bald head, he worked with the boy for hours.

At first it was a splashing battle just to keep afloat. Then

Mark swam his first ten feet, and Clearwater praised him lavishly. After that, his progress was rapid. Finally came a memorable night when he swam from the shore to the boat, a distance of a hundred feet. Clearwater swam beside him all the way, advising him, urging him on. That night his father picked up the hated orange life jacket, smiled at Mark, and said, "I guess you're through with this," and tossed it below on an empty bunk.

During these dull, fishless days they made periodic stops at the small store at Butteville, at the towns of Chenega, Latouche, and Valdez where Mark had made deals with other storekeepers for their old bread and pastry. At each he went ashore, gathered the food into sacks, and carried it aboard the *Far North,* where he stowed it below.

Because no fishing was allowed on weekends, his father would begin cruising toward Orca City on Friday. They always had a few salmon to deliver, and Mark would have a large load of bread and pastry to store in Kelly's cold room.

Mike Kelly had taken to coming aboard the *Far North* and sitting in the galley with Mark's father. They would drink coffee and discuss whether the run was ever going to hit or if this was going to be a lean year. More often than not, when Mark struggled up the stairs with his unwieldy sacks of food, Kelly would meet him at the head of the stairs, tuck a sack under each big arm, and tramp off to the cold room with them.

Mark always saved half a dozen salmon for Ben; and often, as he trudged off the dock with the sack of fish over his shoulder, Kelly would fall in beside him, lift the sack, and carry it easily in one hand. "I'm going uptown anyway," he'd say. "I might as well carry something. You look tired. A rough week, Mark?"

Mark decided Kelly must have a lot of business in town.

The big man was there almost every time he came off the boat with a sack of fish for Ben. But before Kelly took care of his business, he usually carried the fish up the hill and laid them on the Andersens' back porch.

The first time Mark had objected. He explained to Kelly, "Dad says Ben is my responsibility. I should do all the work."

"Your dad's right," Kelly agreed. "And you have assumed the responsibility like a man. As for the work, you don't mind sharing it a little, do you? There's still plenty left to do, from what your dad tells me. And you're really doing me a favor letting me pack this sack up the hill. A man should have a certain amount of exercise, you know. I should climb this hill every day just to keep in trim. But I won't do it unless I've got a reason. Well, this gives me a reason."

Mark explained to his mother how Kelly felt about it when she surprised the big man putting the sack down on the porch. "He's really quite a person, isn't he?" she said, ruffling Mark's straight brown hair.

"Yes," Mark said. "He says they get a silver salmon now and then in a load of pinks, and they can't can them. So he's going to put them in the cold room for Ben this winter."

Ten days before the season was to end, the run suddenly hit again. It was during this time that Mark saw the pirate boat. They were returning from Orca City, where they had delivered a load of salmon, and were cruising off Constantine Harbor early one morning. In the distance Clearwater spotted the gray-and-black shape of a boat against a bank. It was partially hidden by overhanging brush.

"A pirate with a full load on, sure as shootin'," Clearwater said, studying the boat through the glasses.

Mark's father looked, and agreed. "I know that boat."

Mark asked excitedly if he could see, and his father handed him the glasses.

Through the powerful lenses the pirate boat jumped close, clear in every detail. She lay low in the water, a sure sign she was loaded with fish. A man was taking down sacks from over the pilothouse windows. Sacks hung over the bow, hiding the nameplate. The man taking down the sacks turned and glanced toward the *Far North,* and Mark saw the dark, blunt features, the wide, thick-lipped mouth.

"Dad!" he cried excitedly, "it's Fog Benson!"

"I know," Kark Andersen said grimly.

Clearwater shoved back his beret and said: "It was foggy last night, and kind of dark. Perfect for a pirate to lift a trap. He ain't come far from the trap this early in the mornin'. What's the most logical trap to lift around here?"

"Six-Fathom Johnson's Windy Point pile trap," Mark's father said. "The trap shack's on shore two hundred yards away. Perfect for a pirate."

"If they know he did it, why can't they arrest him?" Mark asked.

"Knowin' and provin' are two different things," Clearwater answered. "Probably nobody saw him rob the trap, or if they did, won't say so because he bought 'em off. And once the fish are in the hold of a pirate boat, there's no way to identify 'em as comin' from any certain trap."

"How does a pirate rob a trap, Clearwater?"

"He operates best on dark or foggy nights. He'll block out the windows of his boat so no light shows, and cover up the nameplate when he sneaks up on the trap. If he's clever and quiet, he might dip out every fish in the trap without wakin' the watchmen. Or he might make a deal with the watchmen: buy 'em off by offerin' them five or ten cents a fish for all they'll let him steal. The watchmen then just stay in the shack and see nothin' and hear nothin' durin' the robbery. The pirate can slip the money under the door as he leaves."

"What if the watchmen refuse to sell to the pirates?"

"In that case, if the pirate really wants the fish bad, he'll sneak in, fire a couple of shots through the trap-shack roof. He'll yell at the watchmen, warnin' them not to come out. Then he stands guard with a rifle while his crew robs the trap."

"Has Fog Benson shot at watchmen?"

"They say he has."

Mark bet he would. Anyone who would be mean to Ben, who'd half starve him for almost five years, would do anything.

An hour later they pulled in to the Windy Point trap. The two watchmen and Six-Fathom Johnson were standing on the trap walkway, surveying the damage the pirate had done. The netting of the spiller was slashed to ribbons where the pirate had cut it to get at the trapped salmon.

Johnson came to meet them. He was a tall, rawboned old man with a great shock of snow-white hair. "They lifted my trap last night," he yelled angrily, waving a long, lean arm. "There was ten thousand in th' spiller, and now there ain't one. Ten thousand, gone like that!" He snapped his long fingers. "And look at that spiller. Slashed it with a knife to get at 'em. Five hundred dollars damage, if it's a cent. It'll take at least two days to patch it. Two days fishin' I lose."

Clearwater said, "We spotted Fog Benson takin' sacks off his pilothouse windows about an hour back. He had a big load."

Johnson nodded ponderously. "I figured that's who it was. He's took me before. I know it, but I can't prove it." He lowered his voice and tipped his white head toward his two watchmen. "I can't prove they sold out to him last night either, but I know that, too. I'll bet they've got a thousand dollars cash stashed around here someplace."

"How did you get here so soon?" Mark's father asked.

"Oh, they called th' cannery short wave early this mornin' and reported it, all innocent an' everythin'. Th' cannery called me, an' I come out by boat. I just got to sell this trap, Karl. I'm too old t' guard it myself, an' I can't seem t' hire honest watchmen."

"I know," Mark's father said. "It's a good trap. One of the best in the Sound. If I didn't have the *Far North*—"

"I'd rather you had it than anybody else," Johnson said. "Your daddy an' me was good friends. You been a good friend, too. But I understand. Oh, well, maybe somebody else'll buy it. Anyway, I might as well finish out th' season with these two. It's too late t' hunt for new watchmen and they won't dare sell 'em all t' Benson, so I'll make a little somethin'. You hear of anybody wants to buy a good trap, tell 'em, huh?"

"I'll do that."

The *Far North* backed from the Windy Point trap and resumed combing the sea for salmon.

They got two more big loads and wound up with a smaller one.

The season ended as quickly as it had begun. On the last day, they were cruising off Bligh Island, hoping for one more set. Mark was spotting alone on top of the pilothouse when his father called out from below, "Six o'clock, Mark. The season just ended. Come on down."

It had been a good season for Karl Andersen and the crew of the *Far North*. They had come in with seven big loads and two half loads. They had made their year's wages in one short month.

"That's seinin'," Clearwater said. "You make it big, or go hungry all year and borrow from the cannery to live. Then hope to pay it back next season."

The end of the fishing season brought swift changes in the North. Almost overnight the eleven hundred seiners that had come from as far south as Mexican waters disappeared from Orca City's bay and from the Sound. Suddenly there were only a dozen or so boats left in the harbor. Up and down the coast the canneries' doors closed. Oceangoing ships stopped at each cannery, and the year's catch was loaded aboard for transport to the States. The floating traps were hauled from their locations at sea and left on the beaches for the winter. The pilings were pulled from the sea's bottom to leave the location clear for navigation. The hundreds of cannery workers who had jammed Orca City's one mud and boardwalk street left by boat and plane. Once again Orca City was a small, almost deserted fishing village of some three or four hundred persons.

Ellen took Mark to Dr. Walker. He had grown an inch and added ten pounds. He was brown and tough. "A good healthy specimen and ready for winter," Dr. Walker said.

Ben had also grown. He had added several hundred pounds, and his coat was sleek and taffy-gold. He, too, was well prepared for his winter sleep.

Mark had done exceptionally well in his food collections for Ben. He had a huge pile of bread and old pastries packed into Mike Kelly's cold room at Northern Fisheries. And, true to his promise, Mike Kelly had frozen thirty-nine extra silver salmon that had got into the nets. Mark thanked Kelly, and offered to work a couple of extra Saturdays at the cannery to pay for them.

"Not necessary," Kelly said. "Those were extras, as I told

you. We couldn't can 'em anyway. That Ben is sure going to be surprised when you give him a salmon along about Christmas. I'll bet he's the only brownie in the world that'll get fresh fish when he wakes up in the middle of the winter. That guy not only looks like a king; he lives like one."

Mark grinned. "I'll tell him you put them there for him."

"You do that," Kelly said.

School started. The daylight hours began falling away with astonishing speed. Fall was rushing upon the North, pushed by the long winter months behind it. Geese began going over, heading south in long high-flying V's. Their excited babbling drifted down from great heights. Swans passed over, slow and ponderous, their great bodies and long necks stretched to full length. Ducks congregated by noisy millions in bays and backwaters. They threshed aloft in conglomerate masses, wheeled and returned several times, then, finally stretched out in low, swift-flying V formations that passed the geese and swans. The year-round inhabitants of the North were preparing themselves for the long winter months ahead. The snowshoe rabbits, ptarmigans, the arctic foxes, and weasels were turning white to blend into the white landscape soon to come. A host of other animals, large and small, were hunting dens and burrows in which they could sleep away the dreary winter months.

The alder, blueberry, and willow leaves, touched by fall's first chill, turned rich yellows, browns, and reds, and fell whispering into the long dry meadow grasses until bushes and trees were bare. With surprising swiftness the snow line crept back from the distant white mountains, slinking steadily down canyons, up valleys, and across level plains until once again it was stopped at the water's edge.

Mark had been aware of the approach of winter, but he

paid little attention to it. It was a subtle, steady advance, with no sudden and dramatic change. The daylight hours came a little later each day and disappeared a little earlier. The winds had a tang and bite. His summer shirt and light sweater gave way to a heavy sweater and mackinaw. These things he understood and expected. He had lived with them all his life. But the full realization of winter came the day he ran down the trail from school and burst through the door into Ben's shed.

The new window they had installed gave plenty of light, but he did not see Ben. The chain lay stretched across the floor, and his eyes followed it to where it disappeared in the hay at a corner of the room. There Mark dug down and found Ben, a great taffy-gold bundle curled into a ball. He lay so still, and his breathing was so shallow and slow, that for a sickening instant Mark feared he was dead. Then, suddenly, he knew. He sat there looking at Ben, held in motionless awe by this miracle of nature. The hay was a den. Ben had begun his winter sleep.

ONE morning Cliff Parker lit a fire in the oilstove aboard his boat the *Viking*. The next instant the whole cabin exploded in flames, literally blowing Cliff out the door to safety. The fire gutted the inside of the cabin and ruined the motor.

At dinner that night Karl Andersen said: "Cliff Parker hunted me up this afternoon. He's in a tough spot since that fire. It seems that I'm the only one can help him out."

"Help him? How?" Mark's mother asked.

"His *Viking* is the mail boat, you know. Twice a month he makes that five-hundred-mile swing around the Sound, delivering groceries, medicine, freight of all kinds, and mail."

"Can't he get his boat repaired?" she asked.

"Sure. But it'll take about three months. In the meantime somebody else will have to take his run. His contract calls for two trips a month, regardless. If he misses a trip he loses his contract. He's the only connection some three hundred people living around the Sound have with the outside world."

"That's too bad," she said. "But I fail to see—"

"The *Far North*'s the only boat in the bay fit to take that run."

"He wants you to take the mail run!" she exclaimed. "During those winter storms?"

"It gets a little rough sometimes," Karl admitted. "But it's not too bad. A good boat and a good skipper won't have any trouble." He leaned forward anxiously. "That contract pays a

103

thousand dollars a trip, Ellen. Six trips, six thousand dollars. It's all ours if I take the run for the next three months. There won't be much freight in the winter. It's mostly groceries, maybe some medicine, and the mail."

"That six thousand won't be all profit," Mark's mother said.

"A good part of it will."

"But those winter storms—"

"There are storms in the summer when we're seining," Karl pointed out. "We duck into a hole then, and lay over until they go by. We do the same in the winter."

"There are more storms in the winter," Ellen insisted, her brown eyes worried. "And they're bigger and rougher. And you take chances. Maybe you'll duck into a hole, and maybe you won't."

"The *Far North* can weather anything the Sound can throw at her," his father said proudly.

"There you go!" Ellen said quickly. "Getting risky, taking chances. See what I mean?"

"I said she could take it," Karl said. "I didn't say she'd have to. Good Lord, Ellen, you sound as if I'd go out and deliberately take chances on losing the *Far North*. You know better."

"I don't want anything to happen," she said in a worried voice.

"Why should anything happen? Parker's been making the run for four years with no trouble, and his boat's not nearly as good as the *Far North*. Six thousand dollars for six trips, Ellen. That's a nice round figure." He grinned.

"Money isn't everything."

"It comes in awfully handy, though," Karl said. "Anyway, I talked it over with Clearwater. He thinks it's a good idea."

"He does?"

Mark knew how his mother was thinking. She often said she

was glad Clearwater was with Karl because he was calm and cautious and knew the weather in the Sound as well as anyone. Clearwater, she often insisted, was her insurance that nothing would happen.

She asked, "Clearwater sees nothing wrong with this winter running?"

"That's right."

"Well, all right," she conceded. "Whatever you and Clearwater decide. I know I'm just an old worry wart."

So it was that Karl Andersen and the *Far North* took over the winter mail-boat run.

Mark's mother's fears appeared groundless. They completed the first two runs around the Sound in five days each, with no incidents.

They were not yet back from the third run when the event that was to change Ben's life occurred.

Fog Benson and a half dozen men, including Mud Hole Jones, the big-game guide, were congregated in the Club Bar one rainy night. With the exception of Jones, all were seiners. And, typical of seiners with nothing to do until next season, they were spending their time in idle talk. In the course of the evening they discussed everything of interest in and around the Sound and eventually touched on Ben and Mark Andersen.

"I seen 'em this summer," Jim Patton said, leaning heavily against the bar. "That little kid was leadin' th' brute across't th' tundra like a dog."

"He follows the kid like a dog, too," Ted Adams said.

"That's nothin'. I watched 'im feed th' critter a sandwich once," Charlie Cotton marveled. "The bear ate it outa the kid's hand. No foolin', I saw it."

"I saw that, too," George Robbins agreed. "Who'd ever thought a kid could train a bear like that? A brownie, mind you."

Fog Benson was taking this all in, a scowl on his flushed face, his thick-lipped mouth set in angry lines. "That kid never trained nothin'," he said with disgust.

"Then who did?" Charlie Cotton asked.

Benson prodded his chest. "Who you think owned him for five years?"

"You sayin' you can make that bear lay down, get up, and follow you around like a dog?" Charlie Cotton challenged.

"I'm sayin', if there was any trainin' done, I done it." Benson was half angry at being doubted. "I brought him downtown when he was just a cub and made him drink a bottle of beer." He swung on the bartender. "That right, Sam? Didn't I make 'im do it right in here?"

Sam nodded. "You sure did." Benson had slapped the cub around for two hours trying to make him sit up. The cub had cried piteously. Benson persisted, and had finally succeeded in forcing the cub to drink from a bottle.

"He was a cub then," George Robbins pointed out. "How about now? Th' kid feeds him by hand now."

"Yeah! How about now?" Charlie Cotton wanted to know.

Benson drew himself erect with all the dignity he could muster. "I did it when he was a cub. I c'n do it now."

"I'd hafta see that," George Robbins said doubtfully.

Benson stretched a hand across the bar dramatically, "Sam, gimme a bottle of beer."

"Forget it," Sam soothed. "I saw you do it before."

"And I'll do it now. Th' bottle, Sam."

Sam put the bottle in his hand. "All right," Benson said

with dignity, "you wanta see a full-grown brownie drink this. Come on."

"Maybe he's asleep," Ted Adams suggested.

"So we wake 'im up," Benson answered.

They trooped out and up the hill to Ben's shed, a noisy, laughing crowd bunched in the pale glow of a hurricane lantern.

When they entered the shed, Ben was just waking from a week's solid sleep. He lay, half buried in the hay, staring into the light, utterly listless, his vitality at its lowest ebb.

For a moment the men were struck silent by the size of Ben. Charlie Cotton said, "I knew he was big. But not this big!"

Mud Hole Jones said under his breath, "An honest-to-God trophy!"

George Robbins said uncertainly, "You sure you wanta go through with this, Fog?"

"Stand back!" Benson shouted, and advanced upon the listless Ben. "Get up," he commanded. "Get up, Ben. Up! Up!" Ben did not move. Benson hauled back a foot and kicked Ben resoundingly in the stomach. He kicked again and again, the sound solid and meaty. Still Ben did not move. In sudden rage Benson dropped the bottle and seized the grass scythe hanging on the wall. He jabbed Ben again and again, shouting the while.

The sharp stabs of pain brought Ben scrambling sleepily out of the hay. He retreated the length of the chain, with Benson following, brandishing the scythe. Ben was confused by the light, the strange men standing about laughing, urging Benson on, and Benson's wild shouting.

Benson was enraged by the laughter and at the bear's seeming stupidity. He struck blindly at his head with the scythe. The sharp blade sliced into one of Ben's tender ears, almost ripping off a third of it. The searing pain brought the bear suddenly wide awake. With unbelievable speed he was on Benson with a full-throated roar of rage. His great claw-studded paw lashed out, ripping into Benson's face. It lifted and hurled him across the shed, where he crashed against the wall, a senseless, bloody wreck.

There was sudden silence. Ben stood reared on hind legs to his great, imposing height. The flickering lantern light threw shadows over his huge form until he looked like some prehistoric monster from another world. He swung his great head, growling ominously, the sound like the rumble of distant thunder.

The men backed toward the door. Mud Hole Jones bent over the unconscious Benson and said, "We got to get him to a doctor quick. His face is a mess." The sudden violence had sobered them. They gathered up Benson, making a cradle of their arms, and carried him hurriedly down the trail to town.

Ben's roar of rage had wakened Mark. He jumped out of bed and looked out the window toward the shed. He saw the light bobbing down the trail, the shapes of men carrying another between them. He dressed quickly, grabbed his flashlight, ran down the stairs, and let himself out the kitchen door. He sprinted up the trail to Ben's shed.

In the beam of the flashlight he saw the scythe on the floor, spots of blood in the hay, and Ben pacing back and forth, growling from the depths of his chest, snapping his great jaws and grinding his teeth. A trail of blood ran down his broad face and dripped from the tip of his nose.

Mark was starting toward Ben when his mother came through the door, carrying a lantern. She had pulled on a

108

Ben stood reared on hind legs.

housecoat and wore Karl's raincoat over that. She looked very small inside the coat. She took in the scene at a glance. "Mark!" she cried sharply, "don't go near Ben! Stay away from him!"

"But, Mother, his ear's been cut."

"I know." Ellen drew Mark toward the door. "But he's in a killing rage. He wouldn't recognize you or me or anyone just now. We've got to let him cool down." She glanced about. "I wonder what happened? That noise woke me. I saw men going down the trail carrying another man. Do you know who it was?"

"I couldn't see," Mark said.

"Whoever it was cut Ben with the scythe," she said. "Then Ben attacked him. Oh, Lord! I hope the man's not dead. But what were they doing here?"

"I don't know," Mark said.

Ben kept grinding his teeth, rumbling angrily, and snapping his jaws.

Ellen watched Ben and said, "Run down and get a pan of water and some rags from the rag bag. When he quiets down, we'll try to clean him up."

His mother was still watching Ben from the doorway when Mark returned. They eased inside, set the water and rags on the floor, and hung the lantern from a nail.

They were still watching Ben and were not aware of the men until they came through the door. Mark knew them all. The bandy-legged little man in the lead who carried a rifle was Mud Hole Jones.

"What do you want?" Mark's mother demanded.

Her presence startled them. For a moment they were confused. Mud Hole Jones recovered first. "I sure am sorry to tell you this, Missus Andersen," he said, "but that bear, that Ben, attacked Fog Benson and almost killed him. Fact is, he might be dead for all we know."

Mark's mother waited.

"We can't have that happenin'," Jones defended. "It's just too dangerous havin' this bear around so close to town."

"I see." Mark's mother kept looking at Jones.

"We don't like to do this," Jones explained. "We had a meetin' and we—we talked it over. We got no choice."

"You have a choice," Mark's mother said coldly. "You can get out of here."

"We're doin' this for your own safety as well as for the rest of the town," Charlie Cotton insisted.

"We'll take care of ourselves," Mark's mother said angrily. "Now get out."

Jones shook his head stubbornly. "I'm sorry, ma'am. We can't do that. If you'll just take the boy outside—"

"You can't!" Mark shouted. "You can't! Mother!"

"Be quiet, Mark," his mother said in a calm voice. She faced the men, arms folded, her dark head high, her chin lifted. She had never looked so calm, so small, so self-possessed. She spoke to them as she would to an unruly class of schoolchildren. "You are not going to shoot anything. Is that understood?"

Mud Hole Jones was at a loss. He shifted the rifle uncomfortably. "I'm sorry, ma'am. But Fog Benson—"

"What was he doing here? He cut Ben with the scythe, didn't he? What were you *all* doing here?" she demanded.

"That ain't important now."

"It certainly is! And Karl Andersen is going to ask that same question when he gets home."

There was a commotion at the door, and the huge figure of Mike Kelly strode into the light. He looked at Jones, then reached out, took the rifle, and sent him flying against the far wall with a violent shove.

"Mike!" Mark cried, "they want to shoot Ben!"

Kelly fixed the men with black, unfriendly eyes. "I know. I was in the back booth at the Club Bar when they decided this. Very brave men. They'd like to make the laws."

Jones came back rubbing his arm. He said in a placating voice, "You know what happened. Then you know this's gotta be done."

"Nothing's got to be done."

"That bear almost killed Benson," Charlie Cotton said.

"That's bad? Now, get this straight," Kelly said bluntly. "Nothing's going to be done until Karl Andersen gets home. Then, if something is done, he'll decide it and do it. Now you can go back to the bar and hold another meeting. And one other thing"—his black eyes challenged them with so direct a look no man could meet it—"don't try sneaking up during the night, because I'll be here and I'll stomp you out of sight in the mud. Now get out!"

Mud Hole Jones said, "You ain't heard th' last of this." He held out a hand. "I'll take my rifle."

"You will when I give it to you," Kelly snapped. "Get!"

When they had gone, Mark's mother rubbed a hand across her eyes. "I'm so glad you came. I'm so glad . . ." Her voice faltered, and she began to tremble. "I've never been more frightened in my life."

"Hey." Kelly's big hands steadied her. "You were doing fine. Don't crack up now. Here, sit down while I look things over." He kicked some hay into a pile and Ellen sat down gratefully.

Kelly studied Ben, hands on hips. "Soon as he quiets down," he said to Mark, "we'll try to clean him up. But not now.

112

Maybe we can help him cool off, though. There's nothing like a good meal to make man or beast forget a good mad. Run down to the cannery and bring up three or four of those silvers you've got frozen in the cold room."

Mark's mother asked, "What do you want me to do?"

"It's going to be a long night. If it's not too much trouble, I could do with some coffee."

"I'm staying too," Mark called back from the door.

"You're coming home to bed."

"But, Mother," Mark protested, "I have to."

Kelly said quietly, "Sometimes a man has to protect his property."

Mark's mother rose, smiling. "I guess he does. I'll bring some coffee, and chocolate for you, Mark."

"Now get those salmon," Kelly said. "Scoot!"

Mark returned with three salmon. Kelly cut off the heads, slit them lengthwise and pried them open so they'd thaw quickly. "If these don't help him cool off, nothing will," he said, and tossed the fish in front of Ben.

So great was Ben's anger that for several minutes he padded right over them. Then the scent registered in his delicate nostrils. He stopped and sniffed loudly. He put a big paw on one and ripped out a bite. Suddenly he sat down, held the salmon between his paws, and began eating, growling all the while. As he finished the first one, his growls began to diminish.

When Mark's mother returned, laden with two Thermos bottles and a pair of blankets over her shoulder, Ben was cleaning up the last salmon and had completely stopped growling. But though he no longer rumbled and ground his teeth, he continued to pace. Kelly said, "We'll wait until he settles down for the night. You might as well get some sleep while we're waiting, Mark."

"You'll be sure and wake me?"

"You bet."

Kelly dragged up an armload of hay, punched it down, and said, "Pile on." Mark stretched out, and Kelly spread both blankets over him and tucked in the sides. But Mark was too keyed up to sleep. He listened to the low voices of his mother and Kelly.

When Kelly sat down again Mark's mother asked quietly, "What happened to your son, Mr. Kelly?"

Kelly was silent a moment, then said: "Davey was about Mark's age, bigger and stronger. But they were a lot alike. He could put up a terrific argument for something he wanted, and the crazy turns his interests took kept his mother and me hopping. But he was a good kid.

"That last summer, three years ago, I couldn't get away, so I sent them up to Spirit Lake alone for a vacation. They apparently went out in a rowboat and something happened. We found the overturned boat. We never did find them."

"That's when you came up here?"

"I stuck it out a few months. But there's no house so quiet and lonely as one that's had a woman in it and a twelve-year-old boy and his friends running pell-mell through it. I had to get away. The company needed a superintendent up here, so I came. This spring I met Mark."

"And it all came back?" Mark's mother asked.

"It wasn't as bad as I'd expected. Three years can rub the sharp edge off a lot of hurt. I can go back now and make out all right. I may do that. They've been wanting me in the Seattle office. Knowing your son has helped me over a pretty rough time, Mrs. Andersen. I'd been running away for three years when I met Mark. Now that's over. I know there'll be times it'll hurt like blazes, but there'll be other times, too."

Across the room Ben stopped pacing. Mark watched him paw at the hay. He stood in it, turned around several times, then flopped down ponderously and stretched his big head on his forepaws with a gusty sigh.

Kelly said: "I think our big friend's calling it a night. But we'll give him another hour. There's no need your staying. Mark and I can hold down the fort and clean him up."

"You'll be careful?" Mark's mother rose, shaking hay from her coat.

"Very careful. You go home and get a good night's sleep."

"I will. I didn't know how tired I was." Her full lips broke into a smile. "I don't know what would have happened if you hadn't come."

"You had 'em licked," Kelly said. "They were about to beat a retreat back to the Club Bar."

Mark turned on his side, and through the open door he saw his mother start down the trail, an erect little figure almost lost in his father's billowing raincoat.

Karl Andersen came in off the mail run in the dark hours of early morning. Ellen told him what had happened, and he went immediately to Ben's shed. He found Ben dozing peacefully in the hay. The blood had been washed from his head, and the piece of dangling ear had been cut off. A narrow strip of adhesive tape protected the raw edge.

In a corner, on a second pile of hay, Mike Kelly and Mark lay side by side, sound asleep. Kelly had the rifle cradled in his left arm; his right was stretched beneath Mark's brown head to serve as a pillow.

Andersen touched Kelly's shoulder, and the big man awoke instantly. He eased his arm from beneath Mark, and the two men walked outside to talk.

Andersen said, "A little trouble last night I hear."

"Nothing we couldn't handle. But that was last night."

"What do you mean?"

"The trouble we get today won't be so easily handled."

"I see."

"The way I figure it, today the good citizens of Orca City start yelling. Their arguments you can't ignore. Want to know what I think they'll be?"

Andersen nodded.

Kelly ticked them off on his fingers. "One: you've got a five-year-old brownie here no shed can hold, if he decides to break out. Two: right or wrong, he almost killed a man last night. Three: this town is full of women and kids and people who are afraid of brownies."

"Mighty tough arguments to beat. What do you suggest?"

"Let them come to you with their solutions. They'll have some. But I see only two."

"What are they?"

"You can take him out and turn him loose. That's no good. The road goes only ten miles out of town, and that's not half far enough. The big lug's apt to come right back to Orca City, looking for easy handouts. The other—" He shrugged. "Maybe we just postponed the inevitable last night."

"Shoot him," Andersen said bluntly. "I've been afraid of that from the very first day." He scrubbed a hand across his face. He was very tired. "I think I'll do as you suggest," he said finally. "Just sit tight and let them come to me."

T HEY came at ten o'clock in the morning, three of the town's leading businessmen and three women who were active in the Orca City school. They sat stiff and uncomfortable in the Andersen living room, waiting for the spokesman, Mayor Henry Beckett, to state their business.

Henry Beckett was a thin, wispy little man in a spotless business suit. He owned the combined drygoods and hardware store.

"Karl, Mrs. Andersen," he inclined his head at Ellen, "we're here on a rather unpleasant mission." He cleared his throat and looked about at the others with him.

"Yes, Henry," Karl Andersen said.

"You know about last night, of course. Benson will live but his face will be badly scarred."

"It wouldn't have happened if that gang had kept away from Ben and the shed."

"No question about that, Karl."

"And Benson provoked the bear. You know that, too," Andersen pointed out.

"I agree with you completely, Karl. Unfortunately, how it happened and why isn't important now. The important thing is, it did happen, and it's made the whole town aware of what it means to have such an animal so close. It could happen again, and with fatal results. We want to avoid that. I know you do, too."

"How would you avoid it, Henry?" Andersen asked.

"You're putting me in an awkward position."

"I'd like to know how you'd do it."

Henry Beckett fidgeted uncomfortably. He did not enjoy this particular civic duty. "Well," he said, "if you were down in the States or near a big city, you could give the bear to a city park or perhaps sell him somewhere. Up here, it seems to us, all you can do is turn him loose or dispose of him. Frankly, we're not in favor of turning him loose. If he were a wild brownie, he'd go off into the hills to get away from people as other brownies do. Unfortunately, he's not wild. At least he doesn't fear people."

"By 'dispose,' you mean shoot him, don't you?" Ellen asked.

"I'm sorry, Mrs. Andersen," Henry Beckett said.

"Why all this fuss about a bear?" a plump woman asked.

"Yes, a bear." Spots of color glowed in Ellen's smooth cheeks. "But he happens to be Mark's pet, Mrs. Peters."

Mrs. Peters sniffed audibly. "Why didn't you get him a dog if he had to have a pet? My Frank has a dog."

"You wouldn't understand." Ellen's brown eyes, almost black with anger, looked over the three men and three women who sat in judgment on Ben. "You're not talking about just any bear now. You're talking about a tame bear, our son's pet, which he loves as much as any of your children love their dogs or cats or whatever pets they have."

"You can get another pet," one of the women ventured. "And at least our children's pets aren't endangering other people's lives."

Henry Beckett said quickly: "We didn't come here to fight or try to bully you and Mrs. Andersen, Karl. We're here simply as a committee of citizens to try to work out a solution to a touchy problem. I know the bear is a pet. I also know that you

118

and Mrs. Andersen"—he bobbed his head at Ellen again—"as fair-minded people can see our point. It's like having a—a dangerous criminal outside your door with him so close to town. We don't want to force a solution on you, and we certainly don't want to take drastic action ourselves. We'd like you to resolve this in your own way."

"You aren't leaving me much of a way," Andersen said.

"I realize that," Henry Beckett agreed. "We were hoping you might have something in mind."

Andersen shook his head. "This has been a surprise to me too, you know."

Ellen asked, "How long will you give us to think it over before you take—take drastic action?"

"We thought a couple of days. I'm afraid the town's not inclined to wait much longer."

"That's right," Mrs. Peters said in a positive voice. "I'm scared right now to let my Frank outa the house." She looked at the two other women, and they nodded agreement.

"You wouldn't consider a new shed and stouter chain?" Andersen asked.

"For this particular bear, no," Henry Beckett said. "Accidents can happen, Karl. And he's just too big and it's too close to town."

"I see. You said two days."

"We thought that should be ample time." Henry Beckett rose. "I'm sorry, Karl. I'm very sorry." He bobbed his head at Ellen. "Mrs. Andersen. I think we'd better go."

When they were alone, Ellen's eyes were bright with tears and anger. "That Mrs. Peters! 'Why all this fuss about a bear?'" she mimicked. "Oh-h-h." She clenched her small fists. "We didn't put up much of a fight for Mark and Ben. What was wrong with us?"

"They were right, and we both knew it," Karl said savagely. "Turn it around and we'd feel the same."

"What can we do?"

"You heard Beckett. He had all the answers. Right down to who pulls the trigger."

"There must be another way. Wait, Karl. Please wait."

"Of course," Andersen said gently. "I don't enjoy the prospect of shooting Ben. But I've been fearing and dreading something like this. We've got two days' grace. But, so help me, I don't know what good it can do us."

"Two days," Ellen said. "Let's use it all. It's not fair that Mark and Ben should suffer for some stupid trick of Fog Benson's. Ask Clearwater, ask Mr. Kelly. Maybe they have some idea."

Karl Andersen discussed it with Clearwater. After an hour, during which they discussed every idea that came to mind, Clearwater shoved back his beret and shook his head. "I hate to admit it, but Henry Beckett gave you the only answer."

"I guess so." Andersen wandered down the dock to talk with Mike Kelly.

They sat in the office. Kelly, chin buried in a big palm, shook his head. "Like I said this morning, I'm afraid that last night we just postponed the inevitable. The more I've thought about it, the more sure I am."

"If you think of anything that might help, let me know."

"I'll do that," Kelly said, and gravely watched Karl leave.

That night Karl and Mark went up to the shed to see Ben. He was awake, so Mark ran down to Northern Fisheries and brought up some bread and another salmon. Mark sat beside his father against the wall and watched Ben eat.

Finally Mark turned to his father and said, "Dad, can they do anything to Ben because of last night?"

"The kids been talking?"

Mark's lips tightened. "Some. Their folks are sort of mad. A couple talked about—about shooting Ben. They couldn't, could they, Dad?"

"I've been meaning to talk with you about that. This is a good place, with just the two of us." His father was using his man-to-man voice. He'd used it a lot this summer aboard the boat.

"I want you to listen and understand. You're getting to be quite a young man. You can understand this.

"People are more than mad, Mark. They're afraid. And fear's the worst thing. It makes people take drastic action to protect themselves. Last night suddenly made the whole town realize that Ben is a full-grown brownie, capable of killing a man. And he is, just a block from town, held by a chain he can probably break, in a shed he can walk right through. It's a frightening thought."

"It wouldn't have happened if Fog Benson and those men had left him alone."

"But it did happen, and it's made the people conscious of Ben's nearness and bigness. They won't tolerate it, son. And when a town decides something, you've got to go along because, for the good of all, they have the right to take things into their own hands. And for the good of all, they say Ben has to go."

"But he's not mean, if you don't do things like Fog Benson did."

"We know that. Orca City doesn't. A committee came up this morning and told us to get rid of Ben—"

"You wouldn't let them take him away, Dad?"

"I've been trying all day to figure another way out."

"What way, Dad?"

"I haven't the faintest idea yet."

"We could build a stronger shed," Mark suggested.

"Nothing made of wood will hold Ben long. You've no idea how much power there is in him."

"We could get a bigger chain."

"Yes. But he'd still be close to town, and an accident could happen that would let him loose. The town people won't go for it."

"We've got to do something." Mark was suddenly frightened. "Think of something. Please think of something, Dad!"

"I'm trying, Mark. Remember," his father dropped a hand on his knee, "I'm on your side all the way in this. I don't want anything to happen to Ben either. Understand?"

"Yes, Dad."

"Good. Now let's go home. And don't mention this to your mother. Those people upset her pretty bad this morning. We'll work this out ourselves."

They went down the dark trail together, his father's hand on his shoulder. Mark felt comforted by the tall, strong figure beside him. His father had said he was on his side. That dispelled all fear. Nothing could stand against his father; he could do anything. He would find a way.

Mark's mother met them at the door. There were spots of color in her cheeks and her eyes were shining. She said in a rush, "Karl, Mr. Kelly has brought Arnie Nichols to see you. Mr. Nichols has a solution for Ben."

Mark would have followed his father into the living room where Kelly and Nichols were, but his mother stopped him. "This is men's talk," she explained. "You stay in the kitchen with me. You can listen from here."

Mark sat where he could look into the room, and listened intently.

Mike Kelly said, "Arnie knows your problem, Karl. He has a suggestion I think you'd better hear."

Arnie Nichols was in his thirties, a thin, nervous man with pale eyes that were never still, and black snags of teeth that showed when he smiled. He had a big old boat, the *Hustler*. People said it was well named, because Arnie kept it busy at anything that would turn a profit.

Arnie said now: "I'm headin' for Ketchikan tomorrow, puttin' the *Hustler* in drydock for an overhaul. If you can fix up some kind of cage for the bear, I got an extra long boom and I can lift him aboard. On the way I'll put him ashore on one of the outside islands. I know a couple where the bank drops right off. I can lay in close an' with my long boom swing the crate ashore, open it, an' let 'im out."

Mark's father said, "That's a fine idea, Arnie. What's this going to cost me?"

Nichols spread his hands, showing his snags of teeth. "A favor for a friend. Maybe you can do me one someday."

"You say you're leaving tomorrow," Karl said. "That only gives me tonight to build a cage. That's not much time, Arnie."

"I've got two-by-six timbers at the cannery, bolts, hinges, all the tools we'll need," Kelly said. "And we can turn on the floodlights to work by. You and Clearwater and I can knock together a cage that'll hold Ben."

"All right," Mark's father said. "I'll get Clearwater and be at the cannery in an hour." He held out his hand to Arnie Nichols. "Arnie, I appreciate this."

"A favor." Arnie showed his snags again.

After they'd gone, Mark's father came into the kitchen and said thoughtfully, "Arnie's no friend of mine, and he never did a favor before in his life. Kelly must have twisted his arm.

Being the superintendent who buys Arnie's fish, he can do that. Sure! Kelly's behind this generous offer."

"Who cares?" Mark's mother said happily. "Ben won't be shot and he'll be free. Isn't that wonderful, Mark?"

"No!" Mark cried. "No! You're not going to let them take Ben away, are you, Dad?"

"You bet I am," his father said. "This is a solution that's dropped right out of the blue."

"But Ben's mine," Mark cried. "He's mine!"

Karl Andersen threw up his hands. "I haven't got time to argue with you. This is the way it's going to be." He looked at Ellen. "You explain it to him. And make him see there's no other way. He's got to accept. No compromises, no changes." Then he was gone.

Ellen said, "Mark, come here. Now sit down, be quiet, and listen carefully. You know the trouble we're in with the whole town over Ben. They've demanded that we get rid of him or shoot him."

"Not shoot him!" Mark cried. "Not shoot Ben, Mother!"

"We won't have to if Arnie Nichols takes him out and turns him loose on an island. Don't you see? Ben will stay alive and free. Think what that means, Mark."

"But I'll lose him!" Mark cried. "Dad said he'd find another way."

"This is the other way."

"But I can't lose Ben," he wailed.

"All right," his mother said with brutal bluntness. "You'd rather have him killed."

"No! Oh, no!"

"That's what the mayor and the town insist on. Mark, you were going to turn Ben loose to save his life. That's what we're

124

doing now. Your father and Clearwater and Mr. Kelly are going to work most of the night building a cage for him."

"But I don't want to lose him," he said forlornly.

Ellen reached out and drew him close. "Ben's an animal," she said gently. "It's not right to keep him penned and chained all his life. If you do, you're not much better than Fog Benson. Oh, you fed him and took him to the creek a few times during the summer. But that's not being free. You've had him all summer and fall and you've had a good time. Yours and Ben's has been a wonderful friendship. But now it's time to let him go. Now you can prove your love for Ben by turning him loose. Freedom is the greatest gift you can give him."

"But some hunters might shoot him."

"They might not, too. Lots of brownies die of old age. Remember, keeping Ben chained isn't proving you love him. It's proving you're selfish for your own pleasure."

Mark knew his mother was right. She was always right. But the hurt of losing Ben was almost more than he could bear. It was a little while before he could answer. Then he asked, "When will they take him away?"

"You heard Mr. Nichols. Tomorrow morning early."

"All right," he said listlessly.

Ellen kissed him. "You're growing up, darling. Would you like to go down to see the cage they're building?"

"I'd rather go up and see Ben."

"You won't try anything foolish, like you did this spring?"

Mark shook his head. "I just want to sit with him, Mother."

They finished the cage that evening, and when Karl Andersen came home he told Ellen, "Mark will have to lead Ben down to the dock and put him in the cage."

"Can't someone else do that?" Ellen asked anxiously.

125

"Mark's always led him before, and Ben goes along. We can't take chances going through town. Henry Beckett insists we have the rifle along just in case."

The next morning when Ellen woke Mark, it was still dark.

Clearwater and his father were finishing their coffee when Mark came down the stairs. His mother said, "You've time for breakfast, dear."

Mark shook his head. "I'm not hungry, Mother."

"All right. When you get back. Put on your heavy coat and cap. It feels like snow."

When he was ready his mother put her arms around him and said: "Remember, you're not losing Ben. You're saving his life. You're giving him the most precious thing on earth, his freedom."

"I know," Mark said. But all he could think was that in a few minutes he'd never see Ben again.

When they went outside, Clearwater carried the rifle. The wind had bite, and pushed against Mark with solid force.

Clearwater said, "Winter's come for sure," and pulled his beret down over his ears.

Ben was awake, and Mark unfastened the chain and led him outside. There Ben stopped, as he always did, and swung his big head right and left as his delicate nostrils sampled the cold morning air.

"Come on, Ben." Mark pulled on the chain.

They went down the dark trail into town, Mark and his father in the lead, with Ben between them. Clearwater brought up the rear with the rifle. Ben padded along beside Mark, only now and then stopping to sniff speculatively at a clump of dead grass or at the base of a rock or stump.

Because Orca City was built on a narrow ledge with the sea

on one side and the mountain rising steeply on the other, there were no back streets leading to the dock. They had to walk the full length of Main Street.

The street was vacant, with only here and there a light in a store window. They passed down the center of the street. Ben moved along steadily with his pigeon-toed stride until they came to the Northern Fisheries' dock.

Mike Kelly had the big floodlight on and was waiting. The cage, made of stout timbers bolted together, stood at the edge of the dock. The drop door was open.

The *Hustler* lay against the dock, her long boom slung out and hanging over the crate.

Arnie Nichols leaned on the rail in the bow. His brother, Sonny, stood by the winch, ready to hoist the cage aboard.

Mark stopped at sight of the cage, and his father said, "Come on, Mark, get it over with. Let's not stretch this out. Put him in before he gets any notions."

Mark looked up at his father. He looked at Mike Kelly standing quietly to one side. He looked at Clearwater. They were all waiting for him. There was no help anywhere.

He led Ben up to the cage door, and there Ben stopped. He sniffed at the cage, stretched his big head forward, and peered inside. Here was something new. His curiosity was aroused. Andersen took the chain from Mark's hand. "Run around in back and coax him in, quick!"

Mark went around and knelt on the opposite side of the cage. He swallowed hard a couple of times, then called, "Ben. Ben." He stretched his hand through the bars, and Ben walked in and began sniffing at his fingers, looking for food.

His father slammed down the door and snapped the padlock in place. "Unhook the chain," he said.

Mark unfastened it and his father pulled it out.

Ben was held fast, but his attention was on Mark and he didn't seem to realize he was imprisoned. Mark scratched at the base of his ears, and Ben pressed against the bars, rolling his big head so that Mark could scratch first one ear, then the other. Mark began speaking to him, his voice low and hurried:

"You're going to be free now, Ben. Really free. You won't have to sleep in any old shed any more and eat the leftovers they throw out from restaurants and stores. You won't be chained again. Ever. You can be out in the sun all day if you like and go any place you want to go. I don't want you to leave, but you have to, because people don't understand about you. I'll never forget you, Ben. Never. I hope bears have good memories and you remember me a little. Will you do that, Ben? Will you?" He scratched Ben under the chin a last time, and Ben stretched his great neck and closed his eyes and grunted like a pig. "Good-bye, Ben," the boy whispered brokenly. "Good-bye." He rose, turned savagely, and started blindly away.

His father was suddenly beside him, an arm around his shoulders. "Son," he said, "I'm proud of you. Very proud."

Mark could not understand what there was to be proud of. He had lost Ben forever.

Clear of the harbor, the *Hustler* punched into the wind and rising seas and began to roll. Inside the wheelhouse Arnie Nichols said, "Sonny, did you lash that bear crate good and tight?"

"I lashed her tight to the railing. Arnie, what island you gonna put th' bear ashore on?"

"No island. We're goin' to Seattle. I know a guy down there that's got a little zoo alongside the highway. He's got a deer, a bob cat, an old cougar, stuff like that. People stop to see th' animals, and he sells 'em gas and postcards and things. He'll pay five hundred for a full-grown brownie."

"But you said you'd turn him loose."

"I had to. Andersen wouldn't have given him to me otherwise."

"Suppose he finds out? He'll sure be mad."

"How'll he find out? Nobody knows but you and me."

"But, Arnie . . ."

"Quit makin' a big thing of it. Look, Sonny, he's just a bear. What happens don't make no difference to him. Andersen didn't have no choice. He was in a jam. We took th' bear off his hands, so he's satisfied. Th' bear ain't bein' killed, so he sure oughta be satisfied. To us it's five hundred dollars for our trouble. That pays our way to Seattle, with some left over. I'd say it was a good deal all around for everybody."

"I hadn't thought of it like that," Sonny said.

"How many times I got to tell you," Arnie said, "you gotta be sharper than th' next guy to get along. You gotta keep thinkin' all th' time. You gotta figure the angles. Ain't you ever gonna learn, Sonny?"

Hour after hour, the *Hustler* slammed into the heavy seas. Ben crouched on the floor of the cage, worried and uneasy. He did not understand this rolling, tossing motion that would not let him stand. The sharp salt smell of the sea was strange. The constant throb of the motor, the slap of water against the *Hustler*'s sides were sounds he had never heard. He could feel the cage move as it strained against the lashings at each roll. What he could not see was how the constant working of the cage was wearing the line thin where it was tied to the railing.

A big sea, a heavy roll, and the line finally parted. With the next roll the cage slid a foot, then was stopped by the slackening line. On the following roll the cage slid back a foot and

129

Ben's great weight behind it shot the cage forward and snapped the remaining lines. It was free on deck.

The deck was spray-wet and slippery. Every motion of the *Hustler* sent the cage sliding. Ben heard the men shout and saw them run toward the cage. The boat rolled, and the cage careened across the deck, scattering the men. It crashed into a steel winch and snapped two of the bars.

Ben was on his feet now, frightened, pushing against the broken bars. The boat rolled again, and the cage slid away from the winch. The men ran with lines, shouting, trying to get the lines around the cage to snub it tight against the rail. Before they could tighten their lines, the cage jerked free, shot across the deck, and struck the winch a mighty timber-shattering blow that caved in one side of the cage.

Terrified, Ben shoved harder against the bars. He felt them give. He lunged forward, calling up all his tremendous strength. The bars bulged outward. He got a paw through. With a snapping and cracking of timbers, his big head and shoulders followed.

Then the boat rolled again, dipping deep into a green trough. The cage sprang back across the deck at a new angle, with Ben's head and shoulders protruding. It struck the rail where it rose only a foot above the slippery deck, teetered an instant, then fell overboard into the sea.

The two men leaned over the rail and peered down. Ben had squirmed out of the cage as it struck the water and was swimming strongly toward a not too distant island.

Arnie Nichols waved his long arms in helpless anger. "There goes our five hundred dollars! There goes our free trip to Seattle. I told you to lash that cage good and tight."

"I did!" Sonny yelled. "I lashed it tight as I could. You looked at it, Arnie."

130

"All right!" Arnie shouted. "All right!"

"Can't we get him back, Arnie? We can catch up with him easy."

"How'd we get him aboard? How'd we hold him without a cage? He's a goner, along with our five hundred." Arnie turned disgustedly back into the wheelhouse, started the engine, and brought the *Hustler* back on course.

The swim to the island was not a long one, and Ben was an excellent swimmer. He made it easily. When he walked ashore, he stood on one of the largest brown-bear islands in the Sound.

The beach was flat, but a few hundred yards back the land rose steeply into mountains that were now blanketed with snow.

For a time Ben wandered along the beach, deserted now by every creature but the gulls. He was free for the first time in his life. To Ben freedom meant only that there would be no Mark to take him back to a shed tonight. There would be no chain around his neck. He could go wherever his fancy took him.

Many wild animals, raised tame, when turned loose to forage for themselves, die of starvation or fall easy prey to the first predator. Not so with Ben. No predator dared attack him. He was older than the days he had known and wiser than the years he had lived. Wisdom and strength from the earliest age of the mammals had been bred into Ben's mighty frame. He was a link to the ancient past, and the centuries behind him throbbed into life with a mighty beat that guided him as surely and firmly as if he had never known any life but that of the wild.

THE first of the winter storms boiled out of Siberia, clawed the length of the Aleutian Chain, and struck the mainland with brutal force.

Mark's father was due to start on the mail run, but he held off, waiting for the storm to pass. He waited four days; with no letup in the weather. He dared wait no longer. On the fifth morning they pulled out, the mail sacks, boxes of food, a new rifle, and a five-gallon bottle of acid for a miner piled in a corner of the galley.

Bundled to the eyes against the storm, Mark and his mother waved good-bye from the dock.

Clearwater gave them a jaunty toss of the hand, pulled his black beret low over his ears, and ducked into the wheelhouse.

On the way home Mark's mother said, "I'm glad Clearwater's along. I'd be worried sick if he weren't."

Five days later the *Far North* was somewhere at sea in the Sound, and the storm had not abated.

It was Saturday morning, and Mark wandered from window to window as he watched the storm drive in sleet-driven gusts for the length of the roughened bay, wash the roofs of the town, and spread across the soaked gray tundra beyond. He could barely see where the tundra fell away to the creek and the bottom land where they had taken Ben last summer to cut hay. The mountains beyond were hidden behind the curtain of the storm.

From the kitchen window Mark asked, "Mother, do you suppose Ben found a good warm hole to go to sleep in?"

"I imagine so." His mother was mixing a white cake, one his father particularly liked.

"As warm as the shed?" he asked.

"It doesn't have to be as warm as the shed. His big body will generate all the warmth he needs."

"And dry, Mother?"

"Perhaps not so dry as in the shed. But if Ben wants it dryer, he'll find another spot to sleep. You needn't worry, dear. Ben is a brownie. He'll do just as all brownies have done for thousands of years."

Mark turned back to the window and said no more.

His mother poured the batter into pans and slid them into the hot oven.

Mark said thoughtfully, "Mother, if we knew what island Ben was on, when we're fishing next summer we could stop and see him, couldn't we?"

"I don't see why not. If you knew what island he was on."

"Arnie Nichols could tell us where he let him off. I'd like to see him," Mark said wistfully. "And just—just make sure he's all right."

"Of course you want to see him," his mother said. "You go right on thinking about it, and next spring we'll see what we can do. But while you're dreaming of seeing Ben, you'd better do something about all that food you've got stored in Mr. Kelly's freeze room at Northern Fisheries. You haven't any use for it now, and it's not fair to Mr. Kelly to keep it there. He may want to shut down the room, but he won't until you get rid of it."

"What should I do with it, Mother?"

"I'd tear the wrappers off the bread and pastry and throw

133

it into the bay. The water will soften and thaw it quickly, and the gulls can have a feast. Why don't you go down and do it now? You're not doing anything else, and the exercise and fresh air will be good for you. Bundle up tight. It'll be cold on the dock."

It was biting cold on the dock. The wind-driven sleet stung like the cut of thousands of tiny knives. It rattled off the sheet-metal roof of the cannery and fell hissing into the bay. The sea gulls didn't seem to mind. In their warm gray and white plumage they paraded about the dock, perched on pilings, and sat in rows along the ridge of the cannery. Others, wings set, rode the frigid air currents above the bay, swooping and diving in roller-coaster rides.

Mike Kelly helped Mark carry half a dozen armloads of bread onto the dock. "When you get through," he said, "come inside where it's warm." He shook the sleet from his black hair and disappeared into the office.

Mark began tearing off the wrappers and tossing the bread into the bay. When the first loaf hit the water, the cannery roof and the dock emptied of gulls. They dived at the floating food in a screaming mob. As loaf after loaf was added to the bay, more gulls came. In a few minutes it seemed that every gull in Orca City Bay was congregated in or above the water at the end of the Northern Fisheries' dock.

Disposing of the bread took only a few minutes. Then Mark stood there, chin tucked into his turned-up collar, shoulders hunched against the wind, and idly watched the gulls fight over the feast. He thought of Ben eating all that food, smacking his lips over every bite, and smiled. He stood there until Mike Kelly's voice shouted from the office door, "Come in out of the cold, Mark."

Kelly's office was big and warm. A desk stood in the center

134

of the room, piled with books and ledgers Kelly was working on. A steel filing cabinet took up one corner. The opposite corner was filled with the short-wave radio and a mike sitting on a small counter.

In the North short-wave radio is as common as telephones in the cities. It is the only means of communication between people when the nearest town may be three hundred miles away and the nearest neighbor a hard ten days' hike. Every cannery, boat, fish trap, plane, fox farmer, and miner has a short-wave set. Mark knew how the airwaves were cluttered up with talk during the fishing season. He had listened, fascinated, when his father tuned in the set. You never knew what exciting news you might pick up. He wondered, idly, how it was during the winter.

He asked, "Is anyone ever on the air in the winter, Mike?"

"Sometimes," Kelly said. "You never know. Turn it on if you like. The switch is right down there at the bottom. Twist those two dials around. You might pick up something. I'll be through here in a couple of minutes; then I'll walk home with you."

Mark snapped on the switch and began twisting the dials as he'd seen his father do. For a time there was nothing. Then a voice said: "Field at Valdez is a mess. Don't try to get in for a few days. I'm over Turnagain now. Be in in another ten minutes." A pilot reporting to his home field. Mark twisted the dials again. Another voice said, "I'm layin' this one out in Macleod Harbor, and I ain't movin' if it takes a week." Another voice answered, "We found a hole in Garden Cove and we're not movin' either. Too bad we can't get together. We might work up a couple of good hands of poker." A pair of boat skippers laying out the storm, and gossiping. Mark twisted the dials again. He picked up a weather report from

Dutch Island, but he didn't bother listening to that. He was reaching for the switch to cut off the set when a voice filled the room, urgent, demanding.

"CQ. CQ. Calling CQ. In distress! In distress! We are sinking! Anyone listening relay message to Ed Wright's flying field, Orca City. . . ."

"Mike! Mike!" It was all Mark could manage. His hand was stopped midway to the switch, his head turned toward Kelly, mouth open on a soundless cry, brown eyes wide with horror.

Mike Kelly crossed the room with great strides, snatched up the mike, flipped the switch and said, "Karl, is that you? Karl? Is this the *Far North* calling? Come in! Come in!" He flipped the switch back, and Karl Andersen's voice came into the room.

"Mike! Thank God somebody's listening! I've been trying for half an hour. Listen, Mike, we're fast on a rock. It punched right through the bottom of the boat and four feet into the hold. We're about a quarter mile south of the Needle and a hundred yards offshore. Get hold of Ed Wright. Have him fly out here and pick us and the mail off. I think he can land with his float plane. We've lost the skiff and can't get ashore. He'd better hurry, Mike! He'd better hurry! Over."

Kelly said, "Karl! know right where you are. I'll personally get Wright on his way immediately. Hold tight, Karl. I'm cutting out now." He snapped off the set, picked up the phone, and said: "Give me the Club Bar. Quick! I want the cab at Northern Fisheries' office immediately. This is an emergency. Understand?"

Kelly reached for his hat. "Come on, Mark. We're going for a ride out to Ed Wright's hangar."

Mark clutched at Kelly's arm. "Mike! Mike!" he pleaded frantically, "is—is Dad going to be all right?"

Kelly patted his shoulder and smiled down at him. "Of course he is. You heard him say they were fast on a rock. They can't sink."

"But he said they were. Oh, Mike—"

"Of course he did, at first. That's so anybody just happening to pick him up will realize immediately that it's serious, and listen. Come on, leave everything to me. And don't worry. Your dad's going to be all right. This's old Mike telling you, son."

They were waiting outside in the driving sleet when the cab skidded to a stop a minute later.

In the cab Mark asked, "Will Dad lose the *Far North?* Will she be smashed on the rock?"

"There's no telling. If she's stuck fast enough and can last out the storm, maybe she can be lifted off in good weather."

"But if there's a hole in the bottom water's getting inside." In Mark's mind when water began pouring through a hole into a boat, the boat was doomed.

"The *Far North*'s got pumps," Kelly pointed out. "You know about pumps to pump water out of a boat, I'm sure. Well, you can bet your dad's got the pumps going and is pumping that water back into the sea as fast as it's coming in, maybe faster."

Of course. He'd forgotten about the pumps.

Ed Wright's flying field was a mile out of town on the shore of a small lake. It consisted of a single plane hangar and one yellow twin-motored plane on floats. It was protected from the storm by a three-hundred-foot-high mountain.

The plane was staked out near the shore. Ed Wright was preparing to nail down a section of sheet-iron roof that was leaking.

Kelly gave Wright the story fast.

137

Wright dropped his hammer, snatched up a jacket, and ran for the plane. Five minutes later the yellow plane roared the length of the lake, rose, and headed into the teeth of the storm.

Kelly and Mark returned to the cannery, where Kelly handed the driver several bills and said, "Go back to Wright's field and wait until he gets back."

"Somebody else might want th' cab," the driver objected.

"Let 'em want," Kelly snapped. "Wright'll be out there in twenty minutes, maybe less. He'll pick 'em up and be back in under an hour. But if he isn't, you wait. You wait all day if necessary. When they get here, take Karl Andersen straight home. Then come here and get his son. Got that?"

"Got it," the driver said. You didn't argue with Big Mike Kelly when he used that tone of voice.

Mark said, "I've got to tell Mother right away. I've got to go home."

Kelly drew the boy into the office. "Wait, Mark, until your dad gets home. Let him tell her. It'll only be an hour. If you or I told her now, she'd think the worst, just like you almost did. It would scare her to death. She might go all to pieces from the shock. We certainly don't want that. So wait here with me until the plane gets back."

In the intervening time Kelly pretended to work on his books, but Mark noticed that he spent most of the time just sitting there, staring at the page.

Mark stood at the window, looking out at the storm. He tried to visualize what it must be like out there with his father and Clearwater. The picture terrified him. He tried to wipe out the picture and think of something else, but he could not. He kept seeing the *Far North* with a hole in her bottom. And they had lost the skiff. They couldn't get ashore. He wondered if Ed Wright would be able to set his plane down in this sea. Planes weren't solid and strong like boats. A cold ball of fear settled in Mark's stomach.

The gulls had finished the loaves of bread he had tossed into the water. They had returned to their perches on the pilings and along the edge of the dock. A few still circled and dived, hopefully searching for crumbs.

Mike Kelly finally came and leaned on the windowsill beside Mark. "They got it all cleaned up, I see," he said absently. "We've got time to get them some more." But neither of them made a move to go to the cold room.

They were still staring out the window at the storm and the gulls when the cab slid to a halt.

"Here you go," Kelly said. "Come on."

"You're coming, too."

Mike Kelly shook his head. "This is a time when families should be alone. I'll see you later."

As Mark climbed into the cab, Kelly asked, "You get Karl Andersen home all right?"

"Just a minute ago."

"How about the *Far North?*"

"Not a stick of wood left, Ed Wright says. And, Mike—no Clearwater—"

"What!" Kelly looked at the driver. "Oh, no!" he said. "No!" He stood there a moment, holding the cab door, black head bared to the storm. Then he closed the door and turned back to the office.

The moment Mark burst through the kitchen door he felt the frightening, oppressive atmosphere. He had felt it once before. It had frozen him into complete stillness then. It did so now.

He closed the door quietly and leaned against it. Neither his father nor mother noticed him. His mother sat at the table,

139

clutching something in her hands. All life and laughter were gone from her face.

His father stood before the stove. He had removed his shirt, and a towel was thrown loosely over his shoulders. He still wore his soaked pants and shoes. A little pool of water had formed on the floor at his feet. His broad shoulders sagged, his viking-proud head was bent, the cotton-blond hair plastered to his forehead. His startlingly blue eyes were dull. His voice was infinitely tired.

"A minus tide and a deep trough in the sea set us down right on that rock. It drove through the bottom like a spear.

"When the plane circled, I stepped outside to signal. Maybe that saved my life. The wave came up under her and lifted her off the rock. I felt her going over and dived off the bow to keep from being sucked under. When I came up she was riding the crest of the wave and flipping over. I saw Clearwater for a second. He had got out of the wheelhouse but he couldn't get clear of the boat. He went over with her. I saw her whole keel. Then a wall of water smashed down on her and drove her under. I never saw her again. Something was floating alongside me, and I grabbed it." He bobbed his head toward the object crushed in Ellen's hands. "That's all I saved from the *Far North*. Everything else is gone."

Clearwater drowned! Mark felt as if his heart had suddenly stopped beating and a great loss went crying through him. He stood there silent and sick and watched his mother spread the object on the table, smoothing and patting it with loving hands. It was Clearwater's soaked black beret. "Poor Clearwater," she whispered. "Oh, poor Clearwater." She pressed her small clenched fists against her trembling lips like a hurt child, and began to cry. It was the second time Mark had ever seen his mother cry. The first had been when Jamie had died.

12

THE final blow of the winter to the Andersen family was the departure of Mike Kelly. He had decided to return to the Seattle office. On his last day Kelly had dinner with them. Then they all rode out to Ed Wright's hangar. Wright would fly him to Anchorage to catch the big plane.

Kelly shook hands with Ellen, and she said earnestly, "I hope we see you again. Keep the past buried as deep as you can. It can hurt you if you let it."

"I know," Kelly said. "It's going to be a little rough at times. But I'll make out. I'm sure of it now."

He gripped hands with Karl and said: "There're a lot of boats around the Seattle area. If I get wind of a good one I'll let you know. And if you're ever down there, my place is your headquarters for as long as you'll stay."

He shook hands with Mark, his big dark face smiling gravely. "You'll be down someday. Every Alaskan comes to Seattle eventually. If you don't come straight to me, I'll . . ." He held a ponderous fist under Mark's nose, scowling fiercely.

"Oh, Mike! You know I will," Mark said.

"Sure you will." Kelly smiled. "You walking out to the plane with me?"

Mark walked to the plane with him and watched as he climbed aboard. The door slammed, the plane taxied out into the lake, and a minute later it was off, roaring over them, fleeing into the winter-gray sky. He strained his eyes, watching the plane out of sight. His small chin was set, but there was a great emptiness inside and his mind kept saying, Good-bye, Mike, good-bye. I won't ever come to Seattle.

His father said, "There goes a man I'll miss."

"We'll all miss him," his mother said. She looked at Mark, standing alone at the water's edge, straining his eyes for a last glimpse of the plane. Mark would miss him most of all. First it had been Ben, then Clearwater, now Mike Kelly, the only real friends he'd ever had. Poor kid, she thought. He's lost enough for one year.

Mark's father continued to search for a boat, but with no success. After another discouraging trip to Ketchikan, where he'd looked at several seiners, he said, "There 're boats to be had, all right. A bunch of rotten junkers that would cost a fortune to keep afloat. When I get into the class I want, it's too much for my pocketbook. There's a tub at Valdez that can be made to run for a while. I may have to take it."

A letter came from Mike Kelly. It was the same around Seattle. Good boats, the equal of the *Far North,* were out of sight in price.

So the winter passed.

Almost imperceptibly the daylight hours began to lengthen. The sun burned the snow off the beaches and off the tundra. Ravines and valleys lost their white mantles, exposing spawning streams and lakes that had lain frozen for months. Winter was beginning its annual retreat to the distant white mountains. The first geese and ducks arrived while the creeks and ponds were still frozen over. A host of large and small animals who had slept the winter months away began to emerge and leave erratic tracks across the retreating snows. Once again the tundra gained its green and yellow hues. In the deep-grassed meadows tender green shoots were pushing through the last film of snow. Soon crews would begin migrating north

142

again to work in the canneries, aboard the traps and boats. Boats would start arriving from the south. Orca City's bay would fill and the town's population start to swell. Another season was on the way.

Time was growing short, and Mark knew his father was getting desperate for a boat. He finally decided on the old one at Valdez, but when he went to buy it the boat had been sold. He was suddenly at a complete loss, with the season only weeks away.

It was then that Six-Fathom Johnson came to see them. The old man draped his lean frame over a chair in the kitchen and said, "You haven't a boat now, Karl. Have you given any more thought to my Windy Point trap? I'd still like to sell it."

Mark's father said: "I'd almost forgotten about the trap. I'm a boatman at heart, and I naturally thought first of finding a replacement for the *Far North.*"

"Think about my trap now," Six-Fathom Johnson said.

"It would cost around $20,000 to drive the piling for the trap," Mark's father said. "I wouldn't have anything left to pay you. I don't know how much I could make with a trap, although I know they're good and that yours is one of the best in the Sound. I guess I just hate to spend all our money on something I'm not completely familiar with."

"Have you got anything else in mind for this season?"

"No," Mark's father confessed. "And I don't have to tell you I'm worried."

"Then I've a suggestion, and you and Mrs. Andersen can think it over. That's a good trap, mighty good. But I understand how you'd want to know all about it before taking the plunge into buying one. It is a lot of money, though I'd sell to you reasonable. But you're right. It will cost about $20,000 a year to drive the piling. Then you've got to pull them out again in the fall. That's another expense. So, here's my suggestion. As long as you haven't anything else in sight for this season, why not go out there as my watchman? I'll make you a good deal: $600 a month plus 10 per cent of the trap's take. Then, at the end of the season, if you like it, we can talk buying terms. What do you say?"

"You're too generous," Mark's father said. "You can get cheaper watchmen."

Johnson shook his white head. "Watchmen are $318 a month. I hire two; that's $638. One's enough, but I have to hire two, hoping that one will be honest and refuse to sell to the pirates. They sold one big load to the pirates last year—that I'm sure of. It was probably 10,000 fish at $0.40 each, or $4,000. That's as much as the 10 per cent I'm promising you. And they may have sold a couple more loads I don't know about. They have in past years. This's a good deal for me, Karl. And it's a chance for you to find out if you want to own a trap or not, and get paid for learning."

Six-Fathom Johnson smiled at Mark's mother, and said: "My wife and I used to make it a summer's vacation when she was alive. That's why I built the trap shack on shore. And it's not a shack. It's a big two-room log cabin. All three of you can go out there, make it a vacation, and get paid at the same time. Think it over, Karl, and let me know."

Mark's father and mother talked it over that night. The season was less than a month away. "The chances of getting a boat this late in the season are practically non-existent," Karl said. "And at least we'd make expenses for the year and not have to cut into the insurance money. That would give me a whole year to look for another boat."

"And after a season you might decide to buy a trap and not a boat," Ellen suggested.

"It's possible," he agreed.

So it was decided. For this season Karl Andersen would become a trap watchman aboard the Windy Point trap. They would all move into the cabin on shore.

Ben emerged from his winter sleep in late May. His great shaggy head burst through the snow cover of his den and he scrambled upward into full sunlight. He shook the snow from his fur and stood blinking his small eyes at the unaccustomed light while he swung his big head right and left as his nostrils sampled the fresh spring air.

When he'd swum ashore from Arnie Nichols' boat months before, he had wandered high into the snow. Two miles from the beach he had found a downed tree. A large hole had been hollowed out when the roots had torn from the earth. It was away from the wind, and the upended roots hung protectively over the hole. There he had gone to sleep. Falling snow had drifted over the den, leaving only a small breathing hole. Ben had spent the remainder of the winter there. It was not so warm as the shed or as dry as the hay Mark had scythed and cured for him. But it was the thing he had instinctively wanted since the day he was born.

Now, leaving broad, snow-packed tracks, Ben left the den and plodded majestically down through the snow toward the beach until he came to the grass line.

His stomach was shrunken from months of fasting, but for several days he required no food. Finally he made his way into a large meadow and there began to feed on the tender new grasses and shoots. Other brownies, just out of their winter sleep, came into the meadow, but Ben ignored them.

His stomach full, Ben finally wandered down to the beach where he had swum ashore months before. There he found the

145

carcass of a beluga whale that had drifted in and had been deposited high and dry. He tasted the flesh tentatively, found it good, and began eating.

A strange brownie emerged from the brush and came toward him. He was big, and the hair along his back was tinged with black, but he was not of Ben's proportions. He padded a circle around Ben and the whale, growling and huffing menacingly.

Ben stared at the menacing new brownie, and went back to eating. The stranger edged up to the far side of the carcass and began eating, growling menacingly all the while. Ben ate his fill, then turned and wandered off. The stranger charged after him a few steps, uttering bloodcurdling growls, as if he would frighten Ben into a hasty retreat or convince himself that he was chasing Ben away.

Ben had much to learn. The years he had spent chained in a shed had made him a complete stranger to the wild. Now, with his first taste of freedom, he set out to explore this new and wonderful land. Day after day, as the daylight hours lengthened and the spring buds burst into leaf, Ben explored. Led by a natural curiosity, and guided by his heritage of keen scent and sharp ears, he wandered far afield. He poked his big nose into odd holes and crannies, drifted into strange ravines and canyons, and climbed hills most brownies would have avoided.

It was on one of these rambles up the beach that his sharp ears picked up a strange sound and his curiosity sent him investigating. A mile later he saw an odd machine a short distance out at sea. It was driving immense sticks into the sea bottom with a *whoosh-stomping* sound. There was a building onshore. It stirred faint memories of the shed where he had lived most of his life.

146

The strange brownie padded a circle around Ben and the whale.

He explored about the building, but discovered nothing unusual. But for a reason his bear mind did not understand, he continued to visit the building at odd times.

A second strange thing occurred late one afternoon. Ben was wandering along the bank of a stream when a great red "bird" roared low overhead. At the last moment he reared upward on his hind legs, jaws sprung wide, great forepaws upthrust as if with one mighty smash he would sweep the bird from the sky.

After the "bird" disappeared, Ben continued following the stream, which wandered quietly through the meadow between low grassy banks. He followed it the full length of the meadow, through an almost impenetrable tangle of alders, and emerged suddenly at the base of a loose shale mountain that rose abruptly out of the flat earth.

Ben began climbing the steep slope. It was not difficult. Powerful muscles had equipped him well for the job, and instinct made him choose the safest, easiest course over the loose rock.

A hundred feet up he came upon a solid ledge of rock that jutted out of the side of the mountain like a tabletop. The ledge was warmed by the sun, and there were even a few bushes growing on it. From the ledge Ben could look down on the valley below. His weak eyes could see none of it. But his sharp senses made him aware of the vastness stretching away below him. It was quiet and peaceful; he would not be interrupted by other brownies. It was a perfect place to sleep away the warm afternoon hours.

Thereafter each day Ben climbed to the ledge for his afternoon nap. Mornings and evenings he spent in the meadow, along the beach, and the spawning stream.

Though Ben saw the dark brownie often, he paid no attention to him. The dark one made threatening sounds at Ben, but the meadow was large and the creek was long. Because there were many places for Ben to go, and he was not yet interested in any particular spot, he ignored the stranger.

One morning some sixth sense sent him prowling toward the creek. There he discovered other brown bears ahead of him. Each had laid claim to a section of creek, and stood ready to defend it against all comers. Ben hunted along, searching for a spot to his liking. He found it down in the flat meadow where the bank was low and grassy and the water fled noisily over a shallow ripple.

He waded out and stood looking down into the clear depths. He was not surprised to see the thin line of torpedo shapes, the vanguard of the salmon run, fighting its way over the riffle, heading upstream to spawn.

He plunged his big head into the frigid water, clamped his teeth into a salmon's back, and marched ashore with his wriggling prize. He dropped it in the grass, put a big paw on it, and was prepared to eat it when, with a roar of rage, the dark brownie charged through the grass at him, ears laid back and teeth bared. He was claiming this section of stream for his own. Ben knew the other was not bluffing now.

This time Ben did not ignore the dark bear. He reared to his full height, forepaws extended, ears laid back, teeth bared. He was ready to meet the charge.

The dark brownie did not hesitate. He plunged straight at Ben. They crashed head on and went down in a thrashing mass, emitting blood-chilling snarls, their teeth slashing. The dark bear bit into Ben's neck and tried to shake him, but Ben's huge paws smashed his opponent away. He charged back, and Ben's massive paw caught the dark bear full on the side of the head and sent him rolling. Ben was on him with a speed amazing in such a huge animal. He bore the other to earth by the sheer weight and fury of his charge. His big jaws clamped down on the dark bear's neck. He heaved mightily, and shook the brute as if he had been a mere cub. The dark one tore free, leaving Ben with a mouthful of coarse fur. But Ben, enraged, was after him now. His great jaws were sprung wide to tear; his claw-studded paws reached to crush the dark one's skull. But the other was through. He was no match for Ben, either in weight or in strength. He turned and ran swiftly away.

Ben now controlled the choice fishing spot on the stream.

Though he had been beaten, the dark brownie continued to hang about at the edge of the brush. Each day when Ben was not on the stream, he would sneak down to fish; but the moment Ben appeared, the other would leave.

No other bear challenged Ben. His great size discouraged attack.

Reared to full height on his hind legs, Ben's head and shoulders would punch through the ceiling of an average room and more than four feet into the room above. His massive jaws could rip a two-by-four in two. With one swipe of an enormous claw-studded paw he could crush the skull of a bull. He was four times the size of a full-grown lion, and his strength was beyond belief. He paced the bank of the stream and the shore of the beach with commanding dignity. His bearing was kingly. With his size and strength he instinctively knew he need fear no living thing—not even man, for man had raised him. That, for Ben, could be tragic. He was now that choicest of all things in the wild, a big-game trophy. Sportsmen would gladly pay thousands of dollars for the chance to bag him.

No one knew this better than Mud Hole Jones, the big-game guide.

150

Jones could not get the picture of Ben, as he had seen him that night in the shed at Andersen's, out of his mind. All Orca City knew that Arnie Nichols had taken Ben out and turned him loose on an island. If Jones could learn which island, he knew a sportsman in the States who would gladly pay big money to bag such a trophy. Jones shrewdly calculated that to such a sportsman Ben's hide would be worth at least several thousand.

Jones waited anxiously for Arnie Nichols's return. On the day the *Hustler* docked in Orca City's bay, Jones went aboard. He knew Arnie, and he was sure he would have to pay for the information he wanted. But he was determined it should cost him no more than absolutely necessary.

He found Arnie alone in the galley and got down to business immediately. He did not want it to get back to Karl Andersen that he had been talking with Arnie aboard the *Hustler*.

He said, "Arnie, what island did you put that bear of Andersen's off on?"

Arnie's pale eyes became sharp. He knew Jones, and in that question he smelled money. "Any number of places I could put 'im off," he said evasively. "Why?"

Because he knew he could not fool Arnie, Jones came right out with it. "I ain't been able to get that brute outa my mind," he said. "I know a man in the States that'd like to bag 'im." He drew his wallet from his pocket. "I'll give you $100 for the name of that island. A hundred dollars for a name, Arnie. Nothin' more." He laid the bills on the galley table under Arnie's nose.

Arnie shook his head, not even glancing at the money. "Nothin' doin'. You'll make a couple thousand off that, maybe more." He smiled, showing his broken teeth. "It's worth $500,

151

if it's worth a cent. Besides, I'm takin' a chance. Suppose Karl Andersen finds out?"

"You gonna tell 'im?" Jones asked. "But $500. You're crazy! The couple of thousand I make won't be all profit. You know that. I got to foot all expenses, keep up a plane. Remember? A hundred and fifty I can stand. Just a name, Arnie. That's all. A name." Then Jones tossed out a shrewd guess, "You let him ashore in my guidin' territory, I know that. So if you don't tell me, you get nothin'."

"You're smart, Mud Hole." Arnie showed his snags of teeth. "Make it $200 and you got a name."

Jones added another bill to the little pile before Arnie. "All right," he said. "Name it."

Arnie counted the bills, slowly, carefully, under his breath, then said, "Hinchenbrook. On the seaward side."

The following day Jones's beat-up red plane flew low over the seaward side of Hinchenbrook Island. He knew every bay, meadow, and stream on the island. He knew where the brownies hung out. If Nichols had not lied to him, Ben should be somewhere close by.

He was skimming low the length of a grassy meadow, following a spawning stream, when a bear rose out of the grass directly under the plane. He had a glimpse of huge jaws sprung wide, great forepaws upthrust to strike at the plane; then he was past.

Jones landed a half mile away on the beach and hiked back into the meadow. He saw the bear in the distance, prowling along the stream bank, and he studied him through powerful glasses. He saw the huge head with a third of an ear missing. It was Ben, and he was tremendous! He was a trophy to top all trophies. For such a one, he guessed, he could easily stretch the price a little. What hunter would complain once he saw Ben?

That night Jones sent a letter to a client in the States, telling him about the biggest brown-bear trophy he had ever seen. He would be a record. If the hunter wanted it, he must get up here in a hurry. Knowing his client, Jones was so sure of the answer that he began packing his gear for a quick trip to Hinchenbrook.

13

SCHOOL was out. Once more the bay was filled with seiners. Orca City's one mud and boardwalk street was again jammed with people who had come north to work the salmon run, when the Andersens moved out to the Windy Point trap.

The trap shack was a big two-room log cabin set back some hundred feet from the water. There was ample room for the three of them. Mark's mother said: "Mr. Johnson was right, Karl. I like this. It'll be a real vacation for me. A woman gets tired staying in the same rooms twelve months out of the year." She had brought along books and magazines to read, and she was knitting sweaters for her two men. "I'll go for hikes and see the country, too," she said.

"You will, after I look around," Mark's father said. "This happens to be one of the biggest brown-bear islands in the Sound. I'll see what we have in the way of bears before you start traipsing off on your own."

"Can I go along, Dad?" Mark asked.

"Not this time. If I run into trouble I don't want anyone but myself to worry about."

"Dad," Mark asked, "do you think Ben might be on this island?"

"Not likely," his father said. "Arnie Nichols was going to put him ashore on one of the outside islands on his way to Ketchikan. Remember? Well, this is not an outside island. Besides, I don't know of a spot along here where a boat could lie in close enough to swing a crate ashore."

The following day his father took the rifle and hiked off along the beach. He did not return until dinnertime. He waited until after dinner before he mentioned his hike. Then he said: "You can go up the beach, straight out from the corner of the cabin. I saw a fox and a couple of deer, but that's all. Keep away from the opposite direction. About a mile down the beach that way, there's a big spawning stream. It runs through a brown-bear meadow and up into the hills. There must be a dozen brownies patrolling that stream and wandering around the meadow. Keep away from that spawning stream and meadow. Do you understand that, Mark? In fact, I don't want you traipsing off in that direction at all."

Later that night, when they were in bed, Karl said, "Ellen!"

"Yes," she replied.

"I saw Ben today. He's up there at that spawning stream."

Ellen sat bolt upright, staring at him. "You're sure?" she whispered. "You're absolutely sure?"

"I'm sure," Karl said. "Same taffy-gold color. And I got close enough downwind of him to see the ear that Fog Benson sliced with the scythe. It's Ben, and he's the biggest thing I've ever seen."

"Oh, Lord!" Ellen said. "Here we go again!"

"Don't worry," Karl said. "Ben stays near the spawning stream with the rest of the bears. There isn't another stream for ten miles, so they won't travel much. No brownie will stray far from those salmon and that meadow full of tender grass. Mark will never know Ben's there if we can keep him away from the stream."

"Has Ben changed much?" Ellen asked curiously. "I'd love to see him."

"He's bigger. I've seen a lot of brownies, but never one as

155

big as Ben is. He looks the same, but much, much bigger. But he won't be the same."

"How do you mean?"

"I mean personality, temperament. He's spent a winter alone in the wild. He hasn't seen a human being in months. And this spring you can bet your life he's fought other brownies for fishing rights on that stream. If I'm any judge, Ben now has the finest fishing spot on the creek. Ben has forgotten his tame-bear days. You can bet on that. He's now a wild brownie in every sense of the word."

"I can't believe he'd forget everything," Ellen mused.

"Well, he has. So don't start getting ideas," Karl whispered sharply.

"Oh, stop worrying," Ellen whispered back. "I'm just thinking and wondering."

"When you start thinking and wondering, it's time for me to start worrying," Karl grumbled, and turned over and tried to go to sleep.

Mark had seen a number of traps while seining with his father and Clearwater, but he had never inspected one close up, and his knowledge of the workings of a trap was very vague. When they rowed out to the trap the first time the next morning, his father explained it.

"Traps have been used in Alaska for over half a century. They're just what the name implies, a device for catching salmon. They're stationed offshore and across the path the salmon swim when they come back to the spawning streams. Salmon follow certain paths through the sea, when returning, and they've been swimming past this point for centuries. This trap is about two hundred yards offshore, and straddles one of those paths they swim. It's made of chicken wire fastened to pilings driven into the sea bottom. The wire reaches from the surface to the sea bottom all around the trap, making a huge corral. The salmon swimming up the coast, looking for a spawning stream, hit the lead, that line of pilings and wire that runs from shore to the trap. They follow it out, trying to go around it, and are funneled into the trap.

"This trap covers about an acre of sea. It consists of five compartments called the 'jigger,' 'heart,' 'pot,' and 'right- and left-hand spillers.' The salmon swim from compartment to compartment, looking for a way out. Each compartment gets progressively smaller. When they reach the spillers, the smallest, they are tightly bunched and are easy for the cannery tender to brail out of the trap into the boat.

"Our job is to keep the trap wire clean of kelp and seaweed or any other drifting debris, such as logs or stumps that might punch holes in the wire and let the salmon escape. We keep track of the amount of salmon coming into the trap, and inform the cannery by short wave every day."

Mark was thinking of last year when they had stopped at this trap. He asked, "Is it our job to keep pirates like Fog Benson away, too?"

"We keep all unauthorized boats from stopping here," his father said. "That certainly includes Fog and his friends."

The morning the season opened, Mark and his father were out early. At exactly six o'clock they cut the rope that held the "Sunday apron" open. The apron unrolled to the bottom of the sea, closing the trap, and the Windy Point trap began to "fish."

The run was not big, but it was steady. In bunches of ten, twenty, or fifty the trap began filling. Two days later, Mark's father called the cannery. Their first load was ready.

The following morning the tender brailed eight thousand from the trap, and still they came.

"It beats seining with a boat," his father said. "The trap goes right on 'fishing' while you're sleeping. I'm going to talk with Johnson at the end of this season. If I can just figure a way to stretch our capital a little."

Mark was on the trap catwalk with his father when the beat-up red plane went over, skimming low along the beach. Mark watched it out of sight and said, "It looked like it was going to land on the beach, Dad."

"It is," his father said. He knew the plane. It was Mud Hole Jones, and he was here for only one reason, a brown-bear trophy. Either he had a client with him or soon would have. They would be sure to find Ben, and the Andersens would hear the shooting in this northern stillness. He said to Mark, "Some hunter up from the States. They'll hunt along the spawning stream I told you about."

"I sure am glad Ben's not here," Mark said. But he could not get the red plane out of his mind. He did not like the thought of any brownie being killed for any reason.

Three days later, as they were clearing kelp from the trap wire, two quick bursts of gunfire floated down the breeze from the direction of the spawning stream. Mark and his father stopped and listened. There were no more shots. Mark said again, his small face sober, "I sure am glad Ben's not on this island."

Karl Andersen did not answer. He was visualizing Ben as he remembered him, nibbling a sandwich from Mark's fingers, padding across the sunlit tundra beside Mark, turning over rocks, the big taffy-gold head and the small brown head of the boy side by side. Mark asleep and Ben stretched beside him, huge, head on forepaws. He remembered Ben as he'd seen him the other day, pacing the bank of the stream with commanding dignity, his bearing kingly, monarch of all he surveyed. Those two shots, spaced as they were, had shattered the vision. A great sadness came over Karl Andersen. He felt that a fine and wonderful symbol of the North had been destroyed, one that would never exist again.

Mark and his father were working a log loose from the wire one afternoon when the gray-and-black boat tied up to one of the pilings. Fog Benson climbed the ladder and came down the catwalk toward them. When Mark saw what Ben's slashing claws had done to Benson's face, his stomach turned over. There were three long scars. The worst, wide and red, began at the hairline, extended down the length of the man's cheek, and stopped at the corner of his thick-lipped mouth. In healing, it had pulled his mouth into a perpetual leer.

Benson asked, "How's fishin', Andersen?" and Mark noticed that the words were slightly slurred because the scar pulled at his lips.

Mark's father said, "Fair," and offered nothing more.

"Tough you losin' th' *Far North* an' Clearwater," Benson said.

His father looked at Benson steadily, his dislike plainly showing. "Fog," he said, "say what you came for and quit wasting our time."

"Well, now"—Benson laughed—"nothin' like comin' to th' point. All right. You lost a good boat. You been tryin' all winter t' find another'n' as good. But you can't. Th' insurance money ain't enough to buy another *Far North,* and you an' me both know it. You ain't makin' much money trap-watchin'. I c'n help you out and add another $4,000 to that insurance money to buy another boat."

"So far you've figured everything," Mark's father said.

"Sure I have." Benson leered. "Now, you work with me

durin' th' season, an' I'll see you get that $4,000. I'll pay you a dime a fish for all you let me take outa th' trap."

"I see."

"You call at ten sharp every night," Benson explained. "Act like a fox farmer or a miner askin' a friend to bring 'im groceries. If th' trap's full of fish an' I can slip in an' get a load, you say, 'When you come by drop me off a couple loaves of bread.' If th' trap's empty or th' tender's due that night, say, 'I don't need any groceries t'day.' I'll know what it means, an' keep away. Simple, eh?"

Mark's father nodded. "Very simple."

Benson's thick-lipped mouth pulled into a bigger leer when he tried to smile. "I was kinda leery of you. I almost didn't stop."

"Saved yourself some time if you hadn't," Mark's father said. "It's no deal, Fog. Get out!"

"What!" Benson was incredulous. "You turnin' down four thousand easy dollars? You that needs it so bad to get a new boat!"

"I was hired to guard this trap. That's just what I'm going to do."

"You're a fool!" Benson shouted. "A bullheaded, gold-plated fool."

When he was angry the scars seemed to become redder, and stood out like painted streaks on his leathery tanned face.

"Get going," Andersen said. "You're wasting our time and yours."

"I give you th' chance t' sell 'em," Benson threatened. "Now maybe I'll just take 'em."

"Don't try it." Mark's father's voice was deadly calm. "Bullets can fly both ways, Fog."

"We'll see," Benson shouted angrily. "We'll just see."

He dropped down the ladder into his boat and pulled away.

Mark's father watched the trap carefully for the next few days. Mark noticed that when he went to bed, the rifle lay on the floor within easy reach of his hand.

The trap filled with another load, and the cannery tender brailed it. Mark's mother said, "That Fog Benson's a big bluff. He'll keep away."

"Fog's an odd one," his father said. "You can never tell about him. I've a hunch he's leaving us alone because he's getting enough fish raiding other traps. As long as he's getting plenty other places, he won't bother us."

The tension relaxed.

A week went by, and they had another load ready. Mark's father called the cannery and was informed that the tender would be out to brail the trap in the morning.

When Mark went to bed, his father and mother were sitting outside, watching the night creep down over the sea, turning it dark and mysterious. In the distance the vague shape of the trap blended almost completely with the color of the sea.

Some small sound woke Mark in the middle of the night. Unaccountably, the darkness within his room was deepening. Even as he looked, it increased. He glanced toward the window, and suddenly started up in bed. A cry froze to a gasp in his throat as complete terror gripped him. A piece of cardboard was silently, carefully being slid over the window, blocking it out. A burst of gunfire rocked the night. The stovepipe rattled as bullets slammed through it.

A bellowing voice warned: "Don't come out! We're takin' th' fish! Don't come out!"

Mark leaped from bed and rushed into the other room. His father was standing in the dimness with the rifle in his hands. His mother was up, and Mark could see that she had hold of his father's arm. She was whispering in a terrified voice, "No, Karl! Let them have them! They mean it. It's only a load of fish!"

Karl Andersen was about to charge out the door, where he might have been killed, but at that moment there came a startled cry of fear and panic, a wild shot—the sounds of running feet.

Andersen threw the door open. He saw the distant shape of the trap, and men tumbling frantically into a rowboat on the beach. These were suddenly blotted out as a monstrous shape seemed to rise out of the earth before him. He saw the silhouette of a great flattened head with small tulip-shaped ears. Then the shape lowered itself again, and Karl could see men rowing wildly toward the pirate boat tied to a piling. He jumped outside, threw a shot at the boat, and then lost all interest in it as Mark rushed past him, crying, "Ben! Ben!"

Andersen swung his rifle toward the shape of the bear, but it was too late. Mark had both arms around the animal's neck and was crying, "It's you, Ben! It's really you! Oh, Ben! Ben!" He was scratching Ben under the chin, half laughing, half crying, and Ben had stretched his massive neck to its full length and was grunting like a pig, with pure delight.

14

MARK'S mother stood in the cabin doorway, smiling at Karl. "So he's a wild brownie in every sense of the word, and has forgotten his tame-bear days. Wanta bet?"

Mark's father looked at Ben, who was near the edge of the trap. Mark had lassoed a salmon with a piece of wire and given it to Ben. Now he squatted on his heels nearby, smiling as he watched Ben devour it.

Mark's father shook his head. "Seems I'll never be right about him. When I heard those shots the other day, I was sure he was dead. I'm glad he's not. Wonder what brought him down here, a mile from the spawning stream?"

"I'll guess that in his bear mind he associates this cabin with the shack where he spent almost five years of his life, where he slept and ate," Ellen said. "It was home. Apparently he vaguely remembers it, and feels an attraction."

Mark and Ben spent the forenoon getting acquainted again. Mark lassoed a half dozen more salmon out of the trap, and Ben ate them happily. Then the two wandered down the beach, Ben inquisitively poking his black nose into holes and around the base of old stumps, looking for something more to satisfy his voracious appetite. At noon they returned to the cabin. Ben lay in the shade of the cabin while Mark ate lunch. His mother had made a raisin pie, and Mark took a wedge out to Ben.

The heat of the day began making itself felt. Ben finally padded out behind the cabin and started off through the brush.

Mark said, "He's leaving, Dad, but he's not heading toward the spawning stream. Where's he going?"

"I don't know," his father said. "He's free. He can go wherever he likes."

"Can't we follow and see where he goes, Dad? I don't want to lose him again."

His father deliberated a moment. "Well, all right." He reached inside for the rifle. "Be back in a little while," he told Ellen.

Ben was in no rush. He lumbered along, sniffing curiously at brush clumps, around rocks, delicately nibbling a bite of grass here and there, but moving steadily off toward the mountains back of the cabin. Mark's father said, "I don't understand it. Ben should be heading for the spawning stream and the meadow like any normal brownie."

Some minutes later they emerged from the scant brush and stood at the base of the loose shale mountain several hundred feet high. Without hesitation, and seeming to know exactly where he was going, Ben began climbing, picking his way expertly over the loose shale. Mark and his father followed, and found the rock ledge where Ben spent lazy afternoons.

Mark looked about. There was ample evidence that Ben had lain up here many times before. He went to the edge of the ledge and looked down the shale slope. The spawning stream boiled out of the mountains behind him and flowed smoothly through the broad meadow to the distant sea. Far off to the left was the shape of the Windy Point trap and the shore cabin. A white seiner cruised several miles at sea. And far across that blue water, the St. Elias Range reared a necklace of white heads encircling the Sound.

Mark said, "Ben has come up here a lot, hasn't he, Dad?"

"Every day, I imagine."

"Is that why those hunters in the red plane didn't find him?"

"Probably." Karl made himself comfortable in the shade of a rock, and laid the rifle beside him.

Ben stretched out in the shade of a bush and rested his massive head on extended forepaws. Mark sat down cross-legged beside him, idly scratching his ears as he stared dreamily off to sea.

He could understand why Ben came up here. It was peaceful and quiet. It was warmed by the sun, and at the same time got the cooling benefit of any breeze. And an animal would instinctively know that the chances of being surprised or found up here were remote.

They remained more than an hour, and the warmth of the rock and the stillness made Mark drowsy. Finally his father roused him and said, "We've got to go. Come on, Mark."

"But, Dad, if I leave Ben now he'll go back to the spawning stream."

"Of course. He's got to eat. It's as natural for him to go to the spawning stream as it is for you to go home for dinner. Anyway, what good do you think it would do to stay with him?"

"I thought when he got ready to leave I might coax him back to the cabin," Mark confessed.

"You don't need to. He'll come."

"You really think so?"

"He came last night. And he's been coming to the cabin pretty regular. I've seen his tracks along the beach. Like your mother said, he probably associates the cabin with the shed where he lived for five years."

"You think he remembers?"

"He remembered you. And the shed was all he'd known for most of his life. He's only been free a few months during the latter part of the winter. Sure, he remembers, and he'll be back. Anyway," his father added, "he apparently comes up here every day. If he doesn't show up at the cabin for a few days, we can always hike up here and see him."

"All right." Mark patted Ben between the ears. "You come see me soon. You hear?"

They started back down the shale slope. They were almost to the bottom when Mark glanced back and said in a surprised voice, "Dad, look!" There, almost daintily picking his way after them, his big head swinging, came Ben. At the bottom he raised his nose, sniffed loudly at Mark's face, then fell in at their heels and lumbered after them with his pigeon-toed gait all the way back to the cabin.

Mark's mother stood in the doorway, smiling. Karl spread his hands resignedly. "Like it or not," he said, "we've got the big lug back again."

Mark lassoed a half dozen more salmon out of the trap for Ben's evening meal. His father said, "We'll have to tell Six-Fathom Johnson you're raiding his trap. But I don't think he'll mind too much." As Ben was finishing the last salmon, Mark's mother came out with part of a cake and put it on the ground before him. Ben immediately left the salmon and bit into the cake.

"It was getting a little old," Ellen explained.

"Old!" Mark's father exclaimed. "You just baked it yesterday."

"So," she said, "I'll bake another."

When Mark went to bed that night, Ben was prowling along the beach, investigating rocks and pools and pieces of driftwood. In the morning, when Mark rose, Ben was waiting for his handout of salmon and sweets.

It was apparent that Ben had no desire to return to the spawning stream to feed. He was doing much better here.

166

But there was no stopping him from hiking off to his rock ledge on the shale mountain for his afternoon nap.

Two mornings later, while Mark and his father were shunting a drifting log away from the trap, the red plane skimmed low over them and settled toward the beach in the vicinity of the spawning stream.

Mark was in a panic again. "Dad! Dad! The hunter's back. He'll be after Ben. What're we going to do, Dad? What're we going to do?"

His father had been watching the plane, too, and now he said calmly: "First we're going to push this log out so it won't punch a hole in the trap. After that, we'll talk it over. But we're not going into a yelling fright. Understand? Ben is safe for the moment. He's right over there on the shore in front of the cabin. Now get your pike pole on this log, Mark, and help me shunt it around the trap."

When they rowed ashore after freeing the log, Mark's mother met them in the cabin doorway. Her usually smiling lips were compressed, and her brown eyes dark with worry. "I've seen that plane before, haven't I?" she asked.

Mark's father nodded. "Mud Hole Jones in with another trophy hunter."

"Jones!" Mark cried. "Then he knows Ben's here. He knows!"

"It's possible," his father agreed. "Arnie Nichols could have told him for a price. On the other hand, this is one of the biggest brown-bear islands, and it's in Jones's guiding territory. There's a lot of brownies up in that meadow and along the stream. Jones certainly knows about the meadow and the stream. It really doesn't matter if he knows about Ben or not. The important thing is, he's here looking for a trophy, and there's no bigger one than Ben."

"We've got to do something," Mark cried frantically. "We've got to save Ben! Jones hasn't any right to come out here and hunt him."

"He has every right," his father said. "Jones is a licensed guide, and this is his guiding territory. When he brings in a hunter to kill a brownie, he's just doing his job. The hunter has every right to kill Ben or any other brownie that strikes his fancy. He's bought his license, hired his guide. He's complied with every law."

"But not Ben!" Mark cried. "He's tame!"

Mark's mother looked at Ben, who was a few feet away, trying to get his big nose inside an empty syrup can as he reached for the last sweet drop. "You're saying there's nothing we can do?" There were angry spots of color in her smooth cheeks. "We have to put up with this?"

"I'm saying we can't drive those men off. They're within their rights. As for doing something, I think we can." He scratched his head, smiling faintly. "A little unorthodox, maybe."

"What?" Mark and his mother asked.

"We can try to keep Ben out of their way. Keep him away from the spawning stream and the meadow. That's where they'll hunt."

"How do we do that?" Mark's mother asked.

"We're doing most of it now. Keep feeding him all the salmon he can eat every day. And those tidbits of sweets you've been giving him certainly help. If there's one thing a bear loves more than sweets, it's more sweets. If he gets all he wants here, he'll have no desire to return to the spawning stream. He's proved that already. He hasn't been back for several days. I've an idea that between all the salmon he can eat, plus the sweets, and his obvious liking for Mark's company, we can hold him here until Jones and his hunter kill some other brownie or tire of looking and go somewhere else."

"But he goes up on that rock ledge every afternoon for his nap," Mark said. "He might forget and go to the spawning stream instead of coming back."

"I doubt it. Food and taste are the predominant drives in Ben's life. He's found both here. He's come back every day since he found us. I'm betting he goes on doing it. Anyway, that's a chance we've got to take. We have no other way of holding him here."

Mark said, "I'll get him more salmon right now," and headed for the rowboat to go to the trap.

Mark's mother made grim motions of rolling up her sleeves. "Ben," she announced, looking at the big fellow, who was holding the syrup can between his paws and running his pink tongue around the inside, "your sweet tooth is really going to be indulged the next few days. I just hope the sugar holds out."

Mud Hole Jones was mystified. He had found Ben in this meadow. He had watched him parading up and down the bank of the stream in his fishing. It was here he had brought his first hunter. It had taken several days to locate Ben, but they had eventually spotted him crossing the meadow from the brush to the stream. They had stationed themselves directly in his path, and waited. Then, surprisingly, Ben had disappeared behind a small rise of land. Jones's client, a young man on his first big-game hunt, had become nervous. When another bear, a large one with an almost black coat, had appeared over the rise, he had killed it. Because the man was pleased with his trophy, Jones had not told him it was not Ben.

Now the salmon run was at its height, and all the bears were eating their fill of salmon, building up fat for their winter sleep. Ben should be here with the rest, claiming the finest fishing spot, gorging himself morning and evening on the choicest food a brownie knows. He should be somewhere around the perimeter of the meadow in the afternoon, sleeping off the full meal of the morning in the shade of a bush or rock. Like the others, between meals of fish he should be feeding on the succulent grasses and roots of the meadow.

For days now they had tramped the long marshy meadow and fought their way through tangles of alders and scrub brush looking for him. They had stationed themselves at various fishing holes, along trails that Jones knew were favorites of brownies, and had waited for hours. Not once had they glimpsed Ben. Not a single sign did Jones find that he had been about. Ben had simply vanished.

After a rugged week Jones was baffled and worried. He had promised his client, Peter King, a record-size trophy, and the tough old man would settle for nothing less. Peter King was an impatient man, and he was soon going to tire of chasing over this difficult landscape without even a glimpse of the bear he'd been assured was here.

This was the first time Jones had guided King, and he was anxious that his client bag a trophy. If he did, King would return again and again. That meant thousands in guiding fees in the future.

Jones had learned much about King. The old man's reputation, as well as his appearance and bearing, awed the guide. King was a tough-looking, husky man with iron-gray hair, an inch or so under six feet. He was head of the very large, very successful King Logging interests. With fists and boots, knowledge and shrewdness, he had fought his way to the very top of his tough profession. He was cross-grained, demanding. He was in the habit of ordering people about and of being obeyed without question. King was careless of his own safety, and this worried Jones. As guide, he was responsible for his client's safety. King had taken up trophy hunting late in life, and he loved to show off his trophies and make speeches about his hunts before various lodges and clubs.

Tonight they were lounging before the tent, resting after another hard and fruitless day's hunt. King said in his dry voice, "You're sure this bear's as big as you said he was?"

"The biggest I've seen in twenty years of guidin'," Jones insisted.

King stretched his legs tiredly and began to rub them. "We haven't seen hide nor hair of anything near the size you say he is. Maybe he's taken off for parts unknown. You thought of that?"

"I've thought of it," Jones said. "It's possible. Brownies are unpredictable. You're never sure they'll do what you expect. But it's not likely he'd take off for other parts. He'd have to travel ten miles in any direction to find another spawnin' stream. And you won't catch a brownie far from fresh salmon durin' the run. They fish mornin' and night, and they stay close to some stream during that time."

The lumber tycoon was listening, and the thought was balm to the guide's ego. He expanded on his knowledge. "I think we just missed him. It's easy to miss one in all this brush and high grass. He could be layin' up sleepin' or restin', and we might walk within thirty or forty feet of him and he wouldn't stir. I once hunted a big one three years before I got him. When I did, he reared up not twenty feet off. Could be the same with this fellow. These big ones get pretty cute."

"You should know. But I can't stay much longer. I've got

business to tend to." King stopped rubbing his legs and stretched out on his back, head and shoulders propped against a log. "Be something to take home a big brownie," he said softly.

They lapsed into silence. Above the towering mountains the setting sun turned the sky blood red; the color flowed down the bowl of the sky, gradually fading until it touched the sea, turning the water from blue to pale gold. It changed the high shapes of the mountains into black silhouettes, and lay thin shadows across the earth.

King's mind was still on the hunt. All his life he had solved problems by dogged patience.

He said, "We've covered a lot of territory the past week. Any we might have missed?"

"None where a brownie might be. There's the stream and meadow and the surrounding brush. That's brownie territory. The rest is those mountains you see a couple of miles back from the beach. That's not brownie country."

"What about those mountains?" King wanted to know.

Jones shrugged. "Just mountains like any others—except for one. An odd shale mountain. But you won't find brownies up there this time of year. There's no spawning streams, no meadows. Nothin' for 'em to eat."

"What about this shale mountain? What's odd about it?"

"It's a couple of miles straight back inland from here. What makes it interesting is that its slopes are covered with loose shale in an area where there's hardly any rock. And about a hundred feet or so up the mountain, a solid ledge of rock juts out from the side like a tabletop. One of those queer things you find sometimes. That's all."

Attention to detail and never taking anything for granted had been two important factors in King's success. Now he said, "Let's go up there anyway. As long as we're here we might as well look. I'd like to see what it's like."

"It's just a loose shale-and-rock mountain some two or three hundred feet high," Jones said.

"I want to see it," King insisted.

"All right," Jones agreed, but he was angry. King was trying to take over from his guide again. "But not tomorrow mornin'. I've got to fly to Orca City for supplies and to pick up any mail or telegrams for you as we've planned. Remember? Soon as I get back, we'll hike up there."

"Good enough," King said.

The following morning, as he was about to leave, Jones made the mistake of giving King a direct order in a voice that sounded pompous and commanding. "Now listen," he said. "With luck, I'll be back in a couple of hours, so you stick close to camp. I don't want you rammin' around this country alone. You might get lost or even chewed up by some brownie. You understand?"

King looked at him levelly, without answering.

After the plane had gone, King strode back to camp muttering under his breath, "Get lost, huh! Chewed up by a brownie. The one we can't find, I suppose. Important-sounding little cuss. What's he think I am, a babe in arms?"

King wandered about camp for an hour, but he was not the sort who could stand inactivity when there was something to do. He was still angry at Jones's commanding attitude. "Little runt throwing his weight around. I'm paying plenty for this trip," he finally growled under his breath. "I'm going where I please."

He got his rifle, loaded it, and headed out through the brush in the direction of the shale mountain.

173

MARK and his father were preparing to take off in the rowboat to clean the trap wire when Mud Hole Jones's red plane flew over, less than a quarter mile out at sea. "Look, Dad!" Mark cried happily. "They're leaving. Ben's safe now. He's safe, Dad!"

His father nodded. "They've been here a week and haven't found Ben or any sign of him. So they're pulling stakes to hunt somewhere else. Jones has to find his client a trophy of some kind."

Ellen had heard the plane, and came to the cabin doorway to watch it out of sight. She was smiling happily.

"Between the salmon and the sugar, we made it. But just barely. I don't think there's a pound of sugar left." She glanced at Ben, who was noisily licking up the remains of an apple pie a few feet away, and said with mock severity, "Don't you ever do anything but eat? I'm sick and tired of cooking for you, you big stiff. Go catch yourself a salmon."

Mark felt a tremendous sense of relief, and he could see it mirrored in his father's and mother's smiles. Each day when Ben had padded off back of the cabin, heading for the shale mountain, they had all listened for the sound of shots. Each evening it had been a great relief when Ben had come ambling back through the brush to the cabin. Mark would rush to the trap to catch salmon for him, and his mother always had something sweet to welcome him with. And so the week had gone, and now the strain was over. Ben could again go where he liked, in safety.

174

"Dad," Mark asked, "Jones won't come back, will he?"

"He could," his father said, "but my guess is he won't. The season when a brownie's coat is prime is about over. Jones will hardly have time to find this hunter another trophy and get a new client in. Besides, he's had no luck out here, so there's not much incentive to come back. I'd say he won't return this year. And now, we've got work to do. Come on."

It was noon by the time they had finished working around the trap. When they finally rowed ashore, the day was getting hot. Ben, his stomach full of salmon and his sweet tooth temporarily satisfied, had taken off for his afternoon nap high up on the table rock.

The Andersens had a leisurely lunch. Mark's mother talked and laughed about the way they had fooled Jones and his hunter and how Ben had diminished her sugar supply. "I'll bet Mr. Kelly would have enjoyed the trick we pulled on Mud Hole Jones," she said. "He didn't like that man."

"And he did like Ben," Mark's father said. "He'd have loved it."

Mark helped his mother with the dishes, after which she curled up with a book she'd brought along. His father called the cannery to report that the trap held a good load of salmon. Arrangements were made for the tender to brail the trap in the morning. He spent some time sharpening the tip of one of the pike poles. Then he retired to the table with pencil and paper. He'd been doing a lot of figuring lately. Mark knew he was trying to plan a way to buy the trap with the money they had.

Mark brought in enough wood for the evening fire, then wandered out and lay flat on his stomach across the rowboat seat, staring dreamily into the clear water. There was nothing to do until Ben returned in another hour or two.

A huge jellyfish undulated its way under the boat. A school

of sea trout darted about, going nowhere in a hurry. A half dozen salmon came by. He watched them hit the lead and turn, following it out. In a few minutes they'd join the thousands in the trap. They'd been gone three years and had traveled perhaps clear around the world and come back here to spawn. Only, they'd never get that chance now.

The sun was warm on his back. The rowboat rose and fell with the gentle motion of the sea. Mark propped his chin on his hands and stared into the depths.

Something startled him. He jerked his head up. His arms ached from hanging over the side of the boat. He realized he'd been asleep for some time. He heard the noise again, rushing down upon him in thundering waves of sound. He looked up, and there was the red plane flashing overhead and settling toward the beach a mile away. He scrambled off the rowboat and raced for the cabin. He burst through the door crying, "Dad! Dad! He's back. Mud Hole Jones is back!"

His mother said, "Oh, no!" and closed her book.

His father said calmly, "He probably couldn't carry everything in one trip, and he's returned for the rest."

"Of course," his mother said, relieved.

His father returned to his sheet of figures.

Mark went back outside. If Jones had returned for part of their equipment, he'd be taking off again soon. He kept his eyes turned toward the spawning stream, waiting for a sight of the plane.

Instead he saw the figure of a man far down the beach, carrying a rifle. As it drew nearer, he made out the short, bandy-legged shape of Mud Hole Jones.

Mark called his father. He came out and stood beside his son. Mark's mother came to the door, the book still in her hand. They watched Jones approach. When he was near, his father walked forward to meet the guide. Mark could hear every word.

"Saw your plane leave this morning and thought you'd pulled stakes," his father said.

"Not yet," Jones answered. "I'm lookin' for Pete King. Is he here?"

"Never heard of him," Mark's father said. "Who's Pete King?"

"My hunter. Left him in camp this mornin' and told him to wait until I got back. Now he's gone." Jones shook his head. "That's the worst man I've ever had up here. Careless, chancy. Tell him what to do and how to do it. You think he'll do it? Not that guy."

"You think he's wandered off and got lost, or gone hunting on his own?"

"He's gone huntin' all right," Jones said worriedly. "He took his rifle. But he might be lost, too. With him there's no tellin'."

"Any idea which way he might have gone?"

"Last night I told him about a shale mountain a couple miles back from the beach. He wanted to see it. Maybe he headed that way."

Mark's father said, "Wait till I get my rifle and I'll go with you."

At the mention of the shale mountain, Mark had eased around the corner of the cabin. The moment he was out of sight, he raced off through the brush. He had to reach Ben before Jones or his hunter did.

After several hundred yards he glanced back. His father and Jones were heading up the beach toward the spawning stream. Mark guessed they would start out from Jones's camp.

The guide didn't know about the short cut. And his father was letting him take the long way around so they would not run into Ben if he happened to be returning to the cabin from his nap. They had two miles to hike. He had only one. He could beat them easily. He began running again.

A few minutes later, as he burst panting out of the brush at the foot of the shale mountain, he found a man lying flat on his back, a huge rock across his leg pinning him to the ground.

The man called, "Boy, am I glad to see you! I've been lying here for over an hour."

Mark asked, "Are you Mr. King?"

"That's right. Who're you?"

"I'm Mark Andersen."

"Oh, yeah." King tried to prop himself up on his hands, but failed, and fell back, breathing hard. "Your dad—runs—the fish trap. Well, Mark, help me—roll this rock off my leg. I can't get leverage enough to do it alone."

Mark got his shoulder under the edge of the rock. King pushed as best he could with his free hand as they heaved together. The rock did not budge.

"We need a pole to pry with, to get some leverage," King said.

Mark found a broken limb. He got it under an edge of the rock, and pried. Still the rock refused to move. He tried prying in half a dozen different places, but the rock was too heavy. He was trying to wedge the pole under another spot when he heard King breathe in a horrified voice, "Oh, God! Oh, my God!"

Mark glanced up, and there, not fifty feet off, was Ben picking his way daintily down the shale mountain, without disturbing a single rock. He had finished his nap and was heading back for the cabin.

178

"Run, boy!" King whispered frantically. "Run! Run! Get outa here! Quick!"

Mark called, "Ben! Ben!" and went toward him.

Behind him, King began shouting hoarsely: "Get away, kid. Get away! *Are you crazy?* Get away from him!"

Mark patted Ben on the head and scratched at the base of his ears and under his chin. Then he led Ben toward King. As the man watched them approach, his eyes were wide with terror. His big body seemed to shrink as he tried to flatten himself against the ground. He was too terrified to understand that Mark was coaxing the bear forward. He knew only that here was the animal he had been hunting for a week—the biggest, most dangerous animal in all North America. And it was padding relentlessly toward him like a tank, its huge head low, its massive shoulders rolling, the epitome of unlimited power and deadly danger.

Mark stopped beside King. He said: "This is Ben. He's my pet. He can roll this rock off your leg. Last summer, looking for mice and grubs and things, we rolled lots of rocks bigger than this. You lay real still and don't move. Maybe I can get him to remember how we did it."

Mark bent over the rock, and lifted. "Come on, Ben," he said. "I can't lift it alone. Come on," he coaxed. He put his shoulder against the rock, and pushed. "Come on, Ben. Help me. Come on!" He got hold of the coarse fur on Ben's neck, and pulled. "Come over here and lift." Mark dug around the edge of the rock with his fingers, making his voice sound excited, anxious. "Come on, Ben. Hurry up."

Ben cocked his big head sideways, mildly interested. Finally he moved forward, his big pads brushing King's side.

Peter King lay perfectly still, his face gray. He held his breath.

Ben sniffed curiously at the edge of the rock where Mark was scratching. He caught no scent of mice or parka squirrels. But he had rolled many rocks in his quest for the long white grubs he liked so well. Grubs had no scent. He scratched experimentally along the edge of the rock. A cleaver-sized claw caught in a crevice. He yanked, and the rock rolled easily off King's leg. Ben sniffed at the ground where the rock had lain, and at King's leg. Nothing there interested him. He looked up at Mark, as if waiting.

Mark said, "You can sit up, Mr. King."

King just stared at Ben, his eyes huge and round. He did not move.

Mark patted Ben on the head and said: "It's all right. You can sit up. See, he won't hurt you. Sit up, Mr. King."

King gingerly raised himself to a sitting position, and Ben tipped his big head forward, looking at him intently. Mark said, "You can pet him, Mr. King. Scratch his ears, like this."

King continued to stare wide-eyed at Ben, as if he were hypnotized. Mark took hold of King's hand and put it on Ben's head. "There. Now scratch his ears. Like this. Scratch harder. Harder, Mr. King."

King scratched automatically. Ben rolled his big head so King could scratch first one ear, then the other.

"See." Mark smiled at him. "He's not wild. He's tame."

"He is?" King asked weakly. "He is?"

"Of course," Mark said, matter-of-factly. "You can see for yourself."

"Yes," King said. "Oh, yes."

"Now scratch him under the chin," Mark directed. "He likes that most of all. Under the chin, Mr. King. There, you see."

Ben stretched his big neck out flat and moved forward until

"You can pet him, Mr. King."

his broad, black nose was almost against King's chest. He closed his small eyes and began making happy grunting sounds. The sounds seemed to break King's trance. As he looked at Mark, the gray color began to fade from his cheeks. He started to smile. "He *is* tame!" he exclaimed in amazement. The full realization came to him. "By the gods of war!" he said in an awed voice. "Oh, by the gods of war! He *is* tame!"

He scratched vigorously under Ben's chin for a full minute before Mark finally pushed Ben's head aside and asked, "Is your leg all right? That was an awful big rock."

"Leg?" King was still looking at Ben, fascinated. "Oh, the leg!" He felt it gingerly. "Not broken. Luckily, the ground was soft. Sore, though." He rolled up his trouser leg and exposed a patch of raw flesh. "Lost a dollar's worth of hide."

Mark helped him up, and he hobbled to the rock and sat down. Ben came up and sniffed at him curiously. King asked, "All right if I pet him again?"

"Of course," Mark said. "He loves it."

King scratched Ben's ears, smiling as Ben rolled his massive head. Then he scratched him under the chin, and laughed outright when Ben stretched his neck and began making grunting sounds again. "By the gods of war! This is something! A tame brownie. A *tame* one!"

As Mark's father and Mud Hole Jones came out of the brush, Jones let out a shout and jerked up his rifle. King bellowed, "Put down that gun, you fool, before somebody gets hurt!"

At the same moment Mark's father struck up the barrel of the rifle.

Karl Andersen came forward. King said, as he continued to scratch Ben, "You must be Mark's dad. I'm Pete King." He jerked his head toward Ben and said excitedly, "Know what

182

this fellow did? Rolled this rock off my leg. Yes, sir, it's a fact. It had me pinned flatter than a pancake and solid as Gibraltar. He just hooked a paw under it and tossed it off easy as flippin' a marble." Suddenly he fixed Jones, who had kept his distance from Ben, with an angry look. "So this's the wild brownie we've been chasing around for a week. Why, he's this boy's pet. He's tame!"

Jones drew himself up to the full of his bandy-legged height and said, with all the dignity he could muster: "He's been out here all winter. As far as I'm concerned, he's a wild brownie. I can't help how he looks now."

"Mr. Jones doesn't understand Ben," Mark's father said. "Neither does Orca City. That's why we had to turn him loose. Now, where's your rifle, Mr. King?"

"Someplace under that pile of shale," King said. "I must have slid fifty feet. Let it go."

Karl said, "I'll bet that leg's pretty sore and you've lost some hide. If you can make it to the trap, we've got a first-aid kit there."

"We'll take care of it back at camp," Jones said stiffly. "Let's go, Mr. King."

King pointed at Ben, who was padding off through the brush. "Where's the big fellow going?"

"Back to the trap for his evening handout," Karl said.

"Then that's where I'm going. I've got to see more of that Ben." He turned to Jones. "There's a movie camera someplace amongst my gear. You get it, and meet us at the trap."

Jones bit his lip to keep back angry words. King was giving orders like the lumber tycoon he was in the States. But because he represented a good deal of money to the little guide, Jones mumbled, "All right," and turned back toward camp.

At the cabin Mark's mother insisted on washing and bandaging King's leg. The old lumberman objected vigorously. "It's nothing. A dollar's worth of hide."

"A dollar's worth of hide can turn into a whole leg if it's not cared for," she said. "Sit still."

When Jones returned with the camera, King insisted on having his picture taken with Ben. As Mark's father said later, "He was like a kid with a new toy."

Mark's father took two reels of color film—all King had—of King standing beside Ben, walking with Ben, petting Ben, scratching Ben under the chin. Mark's mother brought out a piece of cake, and King fed it to Ben in small pieces while the camera whirred.

"I'm gonna show these pictures to my clubs and lodges," King explained. "I'll cook up a regular ring-tailed wonder of a speech to go with 'em. Something like: 'There he is, the biggest, toughest, strongest thing in the whole world on four feet with fur. Practically saved my life, too. Flipped a five-hundred-pound rock off my leg easy as that.' " He snapped his fingers. "Say, Jones, we got to have a picture of that rock, too, and the slide. Don't forget the slide. They'll have to believe me. I'll have the whole proof right there on living film. Nobody can top this for a hunting story. Nobody! By the gods of war, this is really something! Yes, sir. Really something!"

"You're not interested in shooting Ben?" Mark's mother asked.

"Shoot him!" King said, aghast. "I wouldn't harm a hair of his big head." He held up a finger for emphasis. "Know what I'm going to do? I'm going to get rid of all my guns. No more shooting to kill for me. I'm going to bring 'em back alive—on film—from now on. That's a lot more fun. Don't know why I didn't realize it before. A lot of people that never get out to the woods can look at the films and enjoy these trips a little with me. Believe me, I'm going to make those old fogies' eyes stick out back home." He scratched his iron-gray head and smiled sheepishly. "That's a pretty ambitious program for an old duffer, isn't it?"

Mark's mother smiled. "You'll do it. You're the youngest old duffer I've ever known."

King's gray eyes studied her, showing the pleasure the sight of her gave him. "Thank you," he said. "Your husband and son are mighty lucky."

Peter King had a keen, inquisitive business mind, and the fish trap intrigued him. Once they had shot the film, he said he wanted to visit the trap. "Come on, Mark," he said. "I want to see how you lassoed salmon for Ben."

They rowed out to the trap, and Mark lassoed a pair of salmon with a wire. Afterward, his father showed King how the trap operated, told him the history of fish traps, and why they were necessary in the North.

As King looked at the teeming mass of salmon in the spiller, he asked, "How many? And what are they worth?"

"There's about ten thousand in there," Mark's father said. "And they're worth forty cents each."

"Four thousand dollars," King remarked. "How many loads like this will it catch a season?"

"On a big run you might brail the trap every day. But, year in and year out, twelve to fifteen loads would be average."

"Why are you guarding the trap?"

"That's quite a story," Mark's father said.

"I'd like to hear it."

Standing on the trap walkway for the next thirty minutes, Peter King got the whole story of the Andersen family.

King was thoughtfully silent on the return from the trap.

But once inside the cabin, sitting at the table, he began talking. His voice was crisp, decisive, authoritative.

Leveling a finger at Mark's father, he said, "You're wasting your ability and knowledge as a trap watchman. You should own it."

"We've thought of it," Mark's mother said, "but we haven't that much money."

"How much can you raise? Sometimes a man's got to go in debt to get ahead."

"About half," Mark's father said. "We've got to hold back some for emergencies."

"Naturally." King looked from one to the other of them, his eyes sharp and probing. "Always prided myself on being a good judge of men," he said. "That's how I got where I am. Picked good men for each job." He drummed his fingers on the tabletop. "Tell you what," he said suddenly. "I'll put up the rest to buy the trap. I'll take a share of the fish each year, plus the legal rate of interest, until the trap's paid for. Then it's yours free and clear. You got any objections to me as a partner?"

Mark's father's startlingly blue gaze and Peter King's level gray one studied each other for a frank moment. Then Andersen said, "None at all."

"Then it's a deal?"

"No." Mark's father shook his head. "It's too good, too generous. You're doing this out of some crazy sense of gratitude. I want to earn what I get."

"Commendable," King said, "but you're wrong. I'm a businessman. This is a business deal, pure and simple. I'll be getting a good rate of interest on my money, and I'm convinced this trap is a good investment. But, even more important to me—this will give me a ready-made place to come every summer to camera-hunt. I'm serious about that. I've had my nose to the logging grindstone a good many years. Now I can afford to relax and play a little. This is my way of doing it. I like it better right here than any place I've ever been. I'd like to make this my headquarters. Build another room on this cabin for me and my stuff, and it'd be perfect—that is, if you can put up with an old duffer like me. How about it?"

Mark's father smiled. "You've got a deal. But we're getting the best of it."

"Maybe we're both getting the best of it," Peter King said, and they shook hands. "I'll go in to Orca City tomorrow, call my attorney, and start him working on the papers."

"Then it's all settled," Mark's mother said happily. "It's wonderful. It's just—" She made a small gesture with her hands. "It's just super."

Peter King glanced at Mark. "It's not quite all settled. There's one other item of business. We can't write it into the contract, but it's mighty important. Come on, Mark; we'll take care of that now."

Holding the mystified Mark's arm, King steered him to the door and shouted, "Jones! Hey, Jones. Where are you, Jones?"

Jones came up from the beach, still carrying his rifle, and plainly annoyed at being thus summoned. He sidled past Ben, who was tearing the last sugar sack apart, his pink tongue questing for the last sweet grain, and came to the door.

"For Pete's sake," King said annoyed. "You act like Ben was going to tear off an arm or a leg. Relax, man."

"He's a brown bear," Jones pointed out stiffly.

" 'And all brownies are unpredictable, untamable, and dangerous,' " King quoted. "Don't try to sell me that line where Ben's concerned. Anyway, I wanted to tell you that the Andersens and I are buying this trap. The cabin will be my head-quarters whenever I come North. And I figure to spend a lot of time up here every summer. There's a lot of camera-hunting I want to do around this Territory. I'll need a guide and you're it—on one condition."

"What's that?"

"Keep Ben alive," King said promptly. "Don't bring any other hunters in here looking for him. Your job's good, just as long as nobody shoots him. Ben's a personal friend. I expect to see him every year."

Jones did some fast calculating. This would be much more rewarding financially than hunting a trophy for the old man. "He'll be here," he said. "You can count on it."

"I will." King looked down at Mark. "That takes care of Ben's future. You satisfied?"

"Am I ever!" Mark beamed up at Peter King, searching for words to express his happiness. The only ones that came to mind were those his mother had just used, "It's wonderful," he said. "It—it's super, Mr. King."

As Ellen once said, "All the bad times began for us when we lost Ben."

So all the good things began for the Andersens when they found him again. If you should fly over the Windy Point trap during the fishing season, you might see two men down below cleaning the trap wire or clearing away debris. One will be Karl Andersen. The trap is newly paid for, and he and Peter King are planning an even bigger partnership. They will be starting their own cannery operation in the near future.

The second will be Mark Andersen. He's a little older, a little heavier, a very healthy outdoor specimen. But he has the same fine features, the same dreamily wistful brown eyes.

Ellen may not be in sight, but the smoke roping from the cabin chimney tells you she is there.

A mile beyond the trap you may fly over a spawning stream and a deep-grassed meadow. If you are particularly lucky, you will glimpse a great bear parading with commanding dignity along the bank. At the last moment, as you flash overhead, he will suddenly rear to his full heart-stopping height and present a never-to-be-forgotten picture of great jaws sprung wide and huge forepaws upthrust, as if with one mighty sweep he would brush your plane from the sky.

Walt Morey (1907–1992) lived his whole life in the Pacific Northwest and Alaska. He worked as a boxer, a diver, and a pulp fiction writer, and at the age of 58, wrote his first novel about a boy and an Alaskan brown bear named Ben. The book has become a classic.